Christmas
cooking
with kids

Christmas cooking
with kids

Annie Rigg
photography by Lisa Linder

RYLAND
PETERS
& SMALL
LONDON NEW YORK

Senior designer Megan Smith
Senior editor Céline Hughes
Location research Jess Walton
Head of production Patricia Harrington
Art director Leslie Harrington
Publishing director Alison Starling

Prop stylist Liz Belton
Indexer Penelope Kent

First published in 2010 by
Ryland Peters & Small
20–21 Jockey's Fields
London WC1R 4BW

www.rylandpeters.com

10 9 8 7 6 5 4 3 2 1

Text © Annie Rigg 2010
Design and photographs
© Ryland Peters & Small 2010

ISBN: 978-1-84975-024-0

A CIP record for this book is available from the British Library.

Printed and bound in China

Notes

• All spoon measurements are level, unless otherwise specified.
• Ovens should be preheated to the specified temperature. Recipes in this book were tested using a regular oven. If using a fan-assisted oven, follow the manufacturer's instructions for adjusting temperatures.
• All eggs are large, unless otherwise specified. Recipes containing raw or partially cooked egg should not be served to the very young, very old, anyone with a compromised immune system or pregnant women.

• Sterilize preserving jars before use. Wash them in hot, soapy water and rinse in boiling water. Place in a large saucepan and then cover with hot water. With the lid on, bring the water to the boil and continue boiling for 15 minutes. Turn off the heat, then leave the jars in the hot water until just before they are to be filled. Invert the jars onto clean kitchen paper to dry. Sterilize the lids for 5 minutes, by boiling or according to the manufacturer's instructions. Jars should be filled and sealed while they are still hot.

Dedication
To all Santa's little helpers

contents

festive fun!

There surely can't be a better time to get children into the kitchen and excited about food and cooking than around Christmastime. Steeped in tradition and distinctive flavours, there's nothing quite like it. At this time of year, everything takes on a magical sparkle and feels that little bit more special, and cooking and eating are no exception.

Most families will have festive food traditions that have been passed down through the generations – even something as simple as preparing the ingredients for a much-loved Christmas pudding or cake. The simple tasks of weighing and stirring the mixture while making wishes is something that everyone, no matter what their age, can get stuck into. Maybe your

family makes Sugar Mice for popping into the bottom of the stockings hanging at the ends of the beds on Christmas Eve, or edible decorations that add something extra special to your festive home. If you always leave a plate of goodies for Santa and his reindeer as they stop off at your house delivering gifts, why not make some delicious iced carrot-shaped cookies for Rudolf and his chums, and leave Santa a well earned slab of home-made fruit cake? At this time of year, no special touch goes unnoticed.

Festive cooking doesn't have to mean hours spent in the kitchen weighing and stirring. A batch of Peppermint Creams can be prepared in no time at all and, packed into pretty boxes, these well loved

sweet treats make excellent gifts. Just remember not to leave the icing sugar unattended for too long or the consequences could be very messy, as my mother will tell you. She returned home one day when I was little to discover that my brother and I had taken over the kitchen and turned it into a very sticky snow scene!

At this time of giving and receiving gifts, there is something very special about home-made presents, particularly those that can be eaten. A box of Biscotti or bag of Coconut Ice made with love and tied with a beautiful ribbon are guaranteed to bring joy to all those lucky enough to receive them.

There's something in this book for kids of all ages, for those more confident in the kitchen and those just starting out on an exciting food journey. Marshmallow Snowmen are ideal for little fingers to make as they require no cooking or chopping, and for those a little older who might need less supervision, why not bake and frost a Bûche de Noël (chocolate yule log) complete with feathery birds to perch on top?

As this is THE party season, there are loads of dishes that the kids can make to serve to their friends or even to make together for a sleepover. Sausage Rolls and Cheese Straws are always a big hit at parties with little ones, and if they've had a hand in making them, they'll taste so much better.

There are not only delicious goodies to nibble on, but also plenty of ideas for edible decorations, from the very simple such as making a silver Candy Tree tied with pretty packages and threading popcorn into garlands, to the more labour-intensive such as a Gingerbread House, which would make a show-stopping centrepiece for any Christmas teatime table.

This year, start some new traditions with the children in your family. Give everyone an apron and a wooden spoon and let the fun begin.

basic recipes

This sponge recipe can be baked in almost any shape and tin. It can also be used to make delicious cupcakes – just add frosting.

basic vanilla sponge

**medium cake, to fit an
    18-cm round cake tin**
175 g unsalted butter,
    softened
175 g caster sugar
3 eggs, lightly beaten
1 teaspoon vanilla extract
175 g plain flour
3 teaspoons baking
    powder
a pinch of salt
3 tablespoons milk,
    at room temperature

**large cake, to fit a
    23-cm round cake tin**
250 g unsalted butter,
    softened
250 g caster sugar
4 eggs, lightly beaten
1 teaspoon vanilla extract
250 g plain flour
4 teaspoons baking
    powder
a pinch of salt
3–4 tablespoons milk,
    at room temperature

1 Preheat the oven to 180°C (350°F) Gas 4. Grease the cake tin you are using.

2 Put the butter and sugar in the bowl of an electric mixer (or use a large bowl and an electric whisk). **Ask an adult to help you** cream them until very pale, light and fluffy.

3 Gradually add the eggs, mixing well between each addition and scraping down the side of the bowl with a rubber spatula from time to time. Add the vanilla extract and mix again.

4 Sift together the flour, baking powder and salt. Add to your mixing bowl and mix again until smooth and well mixed. Add the milk and mix again. Spoon the mixture into the prepared cake tin and spread evenly.

5 Ask an adult to help you put the tin on the middle shelf of the preheated oven. Bake until the cake is golden brown, well risen and a skewer inserted into the middle of the cake comes out clean.

Timings will vary according to the recipe that you are using.

Here are some of the frostings and icings that are used throughout the book. Refer to individual recipes for further instructions.

chocolate glaze

175 g dark chocolate,   1 tablespoon
    chopped   sunflower oil

1 Ask an adult to help you put the chocolate and oil in a heatproof bowl over a pan of barely simmering water or in the microwave on a low setting. Stir very carefully until the chocolate has melted, then leave to cool for about 10 minutes before using.

glacé icing

250 g icing sugar   2–3 tablespoons water
        or lemon juice

1 Sift the icing sugar into a bowl and, using a balloon whisk, gradually stir in enough water or lemon juice to make a smooth icing that will coat the back of a spoon. Add more water or juice for a runnier icing.

chocolate frosting

**175 g dark chocolate,
  chopped**
**125 g unsalted butter,
  diced**
125 ml milk

**1 teaspoon vanilla
  extract**
**225 g icing sugar,
  sifted**

1 Ask an adult to help you put the chocolate
and butter in a heatproof bowl over a pan of
barely simmering water or in the microwave
on a low setting. Stir very carefully until melted.

2 Put the milk, vanilla extract and sugar in
a mixing bowl and whisk until smooth. Pour
the melted chocolate mixture into the mixing
bowl and stir until smooth and thickened.
You may need to leave this somewhere cool
for 30 minutes to thicken enough to spread.

buttercream frosting

**350 g unsalted butter,
  softened**
**700 g icing sugar,
  sifted**

**1 teaspoon vanilla
  extract (optional)**

1 Put the butter in the bowl of an electric
mixer (or use a large bowl and an electric
whisk). **Ask an adult to help you** cream
it until pale and smooth. Gradually add the
sugar and beat until pale and smooth.

2 Add the vanilla extract, if using, and beat
until combined.

little treats & gifts

Scrumptious, deep, chocolatey brownies that are topped with a delicious chocolate buttercream and scattered with festive sweets.

chocolate brownie squares

100 g walnut or pecan pieces
175 g unsalted butter
250 g dark chocolate, chopped
250 g caster sugar
3 eggs
1 teaspoon vanilla extract
150 g plain flour
a pinch of salt
Chocolate Frosting (page 9)
red and green sweets
edible Christmas sprinkles

a 23-cm square baking tin, greased

makes 16

1 Preheat the oven to 180°C (350°F) Gas 4.

2 Ask an adult to help you line the prepared baking tin with baking parchment.

3 Put the walnuts or pecans on a baking tray and **ask an adult to help you** put them in the preheated oven. Roast them for 5 minutes, then **ask an adult to help you** remove them from the oven and leave them to cool.

4 Ask an adult to help you put the butter and chocolate in a heatproof bowl over a pan of simmering water. Stir very carefully until it has melted, then leave to cool slightly.

5 Put the sugar and eggs in a mixing bowl. **Ask an adult to help you** use an electric whisk to beat until pale and thick.

6 Add the vanilla and chocolate mixture. Mix well.

7 Sift the flour and salt into the mixing bowl and fold in using a large metal spoon or spatula. Add the nuts and stir to combine. Pour the batter into the prepared baking tin.

8 Ask an adult to help you put the tin on the middle shelf of the oven. Bake for about 30 minutes. **Ask an adult to help you** remove the tin from the oven. Leave it to cool.

9 Spread the Chocolate Frosting evenly over the brownies. Scatter the sweets and sprinkles over the top, cut into squares and serve.

These buns are traditionally served on St Lucy's day in Sweden, 13th December, where they call them 'lussekatt'. They are normally made into a backwards 'S' shape, but you could make them into any shape you like. Why not have fun with the dough and make simple animal shapes?

Swedish saffron buns

250 ml milk

a good pinch of saffron
   strands

500–600 g strong
   white flour

1 x 7-g sachet easy-blend
   dried yeast

½ teaspoon salt

50 g caster sugar

50 g unsalted butter,
   softened

100 ml soured cream,
   at room temperature

1 egg, lightly beaten

24 raisins

*2 baking trays, lined with
   baking parchment*

makes 12

1 **Ask an adult to help you** heat the milk in a small saucepan until hot but not boiling. Drop the saffron strands in and leave them to infuse in the hot milk for 10 minutes.

2 Tip 500 g of the flour, the yeast, salt, sugar, butter and soured cream into a large mixing bowl and stir to mix. Pour the warm milk in and use your hands to mix everything together until you get a dough.

3 To knead the dough, first sprinkle a little flour on a clean work surface. Then shape the dough into a ball and push on it and press it onto the work surface, turning it round often. You'll need to keep doing this until it is silky smooth and elastic – this will take between 4–7 minutes and you may need to add more flour if the dough is too sticky.

4 Shape the dough into a neat ball again. Wash and dry the mixing bowl and sit the dough back in it. Cover tightly with clingfilm and leave in a warm place until the dough has doubled in size. This can take at least 1 hour.

5 Tip the dough onto the floured work surface and knead for 1 minute. Divide into 12 equal pieces. Roll each piece into a 20-cm long sausage and twist into a backwards 'S' shape. Place 6 of the buns on one of the baking trays and the other 6 on the other tray.

6 Lightly oil a large sheet of clingfilm, then use it to loosely cover the baking trays (oiled-side down). Leave the buns to rise again for a further 30 minutes.

7 Preheat the oven to 190°C (375°F) Gas 5.

8 Brush the buns lightly with the beaten egg and push a raisin into each end of the buns. **Ask an adult to help you** put the trays on the middle shelf of the preheated oven. Bake for about 12–15 minutes, until well risen, shiny and deep golden brown.

'Lebkuchen' are traditional German Christmas cookies with a good hint of ginger and spices. They can be covered with either a simple white icing or a coating of white or dark chocolate.

Lebkuchen

2 tablespoons clear honey

2 tablespoons black treacle

40 g unsalted butter

75 g dark brown soft sugar

grated zest of ½ orange

grated zest of ½ lemon

225 g self-raising flour

½ teaspoon ground cinnamon

2 teaspoons ground ginger

¼ teaspoon grated nutmeg

a pinch of ground cloves

a pinch of salt

50 g ground almonds

1 egg, lightly beaten

Chocolate Glaze (page 8)

Glacé Icing (page 8)

edible silver balls

shaped cookie cutters

2 baking trays, lined with baking parchment

makes about 30

1 Put the honey, treacle, butter, sugar and orange and lemon zest in a small saucepan. **Ask an adult to help you** put it over low heat and stir until the butter has melted and everything is well mixed. Carefully remove from the heat and leave to cool.

2 Sift the flour, spices and salt together into a mixing bowl, then add the ground almonds. Add the melted butter mixture and the beaten egg and mix until you get a dough.

3 To knead the dough, sprinkle a little flour on a clean work surface. Shape the dough into a ball and push on it and press it onto the work surface, turning it round often. Do this for just a minute or so until smooth, then wrap in clingfilm and chill in the fridge for at least 4 hours or overnight.

4 When you are ready to bake the Lebkuchen, preheat the oven to 180°C (350°F) Gas 4.

On the floured work surface, roll the dough out to a thickness of 5 mm using a rolling pin. Stamp out shapes with your cookie cutters.

5 Place the Lebkuchen on the prepared baking trays and **ask an adult to help you** put them in the preheated oven. Bake for about 15–20 minutes, or until just beginning to brown at the edges.

6 **Ask an adult to help you** remove the Lebkuchen from the oven and transfer to a wire rack to cool.

7 When the Lebkuchen are cold, spread Chocolate Glaze or Glacé Icing over them with a palette knife or back of a spoon. Decorate with silver balls or pipe more glaze or icing over the Lebkuchen with a piping bag. (To make a quick piping bag, take a freezer bag and snip off a corner. Fill with glaze or icing and use to pipe lines onto the Lebkuchen.)

Peppermint creams are one of the first things I learned to make when I was a child and I still love making them now. Once they have dried out, you can try dipping them in melted dark chocolate and scattering with silver sprinkles. Leave to dry on baking parchment before putting in boxes.

18

peppermint creams

225 g icing sugar

4–6 tablespoons
   condensed milk

½ teaspoon peppermint
   extract

green food colouring paste
   (optional)

a mini star-shaped cutter

makes 20–30

1 Sift the icing sugar into a large bowl. Gradually add the condensed milk and peppermint extract, mixing with a wooden spoon. The mixture should come together like dough and you may need to use your hands towards the end of the mixing.

2 To knead the dough, sprinkle a little icing sugar on a clean work surface. Shape the dough into a ball and push on it and press it onto the work surface, turning it round often. Do this for just a minute or so until smooth.

3 If you like, you can divide the dough in half and tint one half green using a little of the food colouring. Knead the dough again until it is evenly green.

4 On the work surface, roll the dough out to a thickness of 4 mm using a rolling pin. Stamp out stars with your cookie cutter and arrange them on a sheet of baking parchment.

5 Leave to dry out overnight before packing into pretty boxes.

This recipe couldn't be easier or more yummy. Look out for wooden lolly sticks in kitchenware or craft shops. Use a variety of edible sprinkles and coatings for your marshmallows. Wrap the finished lollies in clear cellophane and tie with a pretty ribbon.

marshmallow lollies

150 g dark chocolate

150 g milk chocolate

150 g white chocolate

200 g large marshmallows

edible sprinkles, finely
chopped nuts and/or
desiccated coconut

*about 20–25 wooden lolly
sticks*

makes 20–25

1 Chop all the chocolate or break into pieces.

2 Ask an adult to help you put each type of chocolate in a separate heatproof bowl over a pan of simmering water or in the microwave on a low setting. Stir very carefully until it has melted.

3 Push a lolly stick through 2 marshmallows. Dip the marshmallows into the melted chocolate (either the dark, milk or white) so that they are evenly and completely coated in chocolate. Use a spoon to help you finish coating the marshmallows and let any excess chocolate drip back into the bowl.

4 Sprinkle the chocolate-coated marshmallows with your sprinkles, chopped nuts and/or desiccated coconut, then leave to set on a sheet of baking parchment.

These little Italian biscuits are pronounced 'reech-ee-a-relly'. They're chewy and sticky and yummy. You could add a little more finely grated lemon zest or lemon extract in place of the vanilla if you prefer. Dust them in icing sugar, put them in a pretty box and give them to your teacher as a present.

ricciarelli

2 egg whites

a pinch of salt

225 g caster sugar

grated zest of 1 lemon

½ teaspoon vanilla extract

1 teaspoon almond extract

300 g ground almonds

4 tablespoons flaked
   almonds

icing sugar, for dusting

*2 baking trays, lined with
   baking parchment*

makes about 20

1 Preheat the oven to 150°C (300°F) Gas 2.

2 Place the egg whites in a large, clean mixing bowl with the salt. **Ask an adult to help you** use an electric whisk to beat the egg whites until they're nice and thick. When you turn the whisk off and lift them up slowly, the egg whites should stand in stiff peaks.

3 Gradually add the caster sugar, whisking constantly until completely incorporated. Add the lemon zest, vanilla extract and almond extract and mix again.

4 Fold in the ground almonds using a large metal spoon or spatula.

5 Wet your hands under the tap, then pull off a bit of the biscuit dough, about the size of a walnut, and roll it into a ball. Put it on one of the baking trays and flatten slightly. Keep doing this until you have used all the dough.

6 Sprinkle flaked almonds over each ricciarelli.

7 **Ask an adult to help you** put the baking trays on the middle shelf of the preheated oven. Bake for about 25 minutes, or until pale gold.

8 **Ask an adult to help you** remove the baking trays from the oven. Leave the ricciarelli to cool, then dust with icing sugar.

marshmallow snowmen

200 g large white marshmallows
brown writing icing
coloured liquorice strips or fruit leather
chocolate-coated mint sticks (eg Matchmakers)
large chocolate drops
100 g white mini-marshmallows
icing sugar, for dusting

about 10 cocktail sticks

makes about 10

1 Place the marshmallows on a tray.

2 Push 2 large marshmallows onto each cocktail stick. **Ask an adult to** trim off any of the stick that is poking out of the top.

3 Using the writing icing, pipe dots and lines of icing onto the face to make the eyes, nose and mouth.

4 Cut the liquorice strips or fruit leather into thin strips and carefully tie around the snowman's neck for a scarf.

5 To make the arms, break the chocolate-coated mint sticks in half and push into the sides of the large marshmallow.

6 Pipe a small blob of icing onto the top of the snowman's head and position a large chocolate drop on top. Pipe another blob of icing in the middle of the chocolate drop and stick a mini-marshmallow on the very top.

7 Finally, using the writing icing again, pipe dots down the front of the snowman to look like buttons.

8 Keep making snowmen like this until you have as many as you need to make a fabulous winter wonderland!

9 To serve, scatter icing sugar over the serving dish, arrange the snowmen on top and dust lightly with more sugar.

This is definitely a recipe for little hands! These cute chaps are such fun to make and look gorgeous on the Christmas table. Why not make one snowman for each person as a place setting?

This is the kind of sweet treat that your Grandma makes. Make it a day in advance so that it has a chance to dry out before you cut it into small pieces to serve. This would make an ideal Christmas gift.

coconut ice

400-g tin condensed milk
350 g icing sugar
350 g desiccated coconut
pink food colouring paste

a 20-cm square baking tin,
  lightly greased

makes 25–30

1 Put the condensed milk and icing sugar in a mixing bowl and mix with a wooden spoon until smooth. Add the desiccated coconut and keep mixing until the mixture is well combined – it will get quite stiff!

2 Scoop out half the mixture and place in another mixing bowl. Add a tiny amount of pink food colouring and mix well to colour evenly. Add more colour if you need to.

3 Spread the pink mixture in the prepared tin and make sure it is smooth and flat on top. Spread the white mixture evenly on top. Cover with clingfilm and leave to dry out overnight.

4 Cut into squares, diamonds or triangles and arrange in a pretty box.

cranberry streusel muffins

250 ml buttermilk

2 eggs

1 teaspoon vanilla extract

350 g plain flour

225 g caster sugar

1 tablespoon baking
  powder

1 teaspoon ground
  cinnamon

a pinch of salt

125 g unsalted butter,
  chilled and diced

75 g chopped mixed nuts

250 g fresh cranberries

grated zest of 1 orange

25 g unsalted butter,
  melted

a muffin tin, lined with
  12 paper muffin cases

makes 12

1 Preheat the oven to 180°C (350°F) Gas 4.

2 Put the buttermilk, eggs and vanilla extract in a small bowl and whisk lightly.

3 Put the flour, sugar, baking powder, cinnamon and salt in a large mixing bowl. Add the chilled, diced butter and rub into the dry ingredients using your fingertips. When the mixture looks like breadcrumbs, add the chopped nuts and mix to combine. Scoop out 1 teacupful or roughly 125 g of the dry mixture and set aside in a separate bowl.

4 Add the egg mixture to the large bowl and mix until only just combined. Add the cranberries and orange zest and fold in briefly.

5 Spoon the mixture into the muffin cases, filling them almost to the top.

6 Pour the melted butter into the reserved dry ingredients and mix with a fork until crumbly. Scatter evenly over the muffins.

7 Ask an adult to help you put the muffin tin on the middle shelf of the preheated oven. Bake for about 20 minutes or until golden and a wooden skewer inserted into the middle of a muffin comes out clean.

8 Ask an adult to help you remove the muffin tin from the oven. Leave to cool for 2 minutes, then tip the muffins out onto a wire rack to cool completely.

Muffins are super-easy to make and these ones are full of festive cranberries. You could use fresh blueberries, dried cranberries or dried cherries if you prefer.

You'll need adult supervision for this recipe when it comes to making the toffee to coat the apples. Look out for small, red-skinned apples, which will make the toffee look even more festive. Why not try dipping the bottoms of the toffee apples in sprinkles or finely chopped toasted nuts before putting them on the parchment to set?

toffee apples

8 small apples, eg Cox's
300 g caster sugar
2 tablespoons golden
   syrup
juice of ½ lemon
finely chopped mixed nuts
   and edible sprinkles, for
   dipping (optional)

*8 wooden skewers or
   lolly sticks*

*a large sheet of non-stick
   baking parchment*

makes 8

1 Wash and thoroughly dry each apple. Carefully push a wooden skewer or lolly stick into the stalk end of each apple.

2 Put the sugar, golden syrup and 150 ml water in a heavy-based saucepan. **Ask an adult to help you** put it over low heat. Leave until the sugar has completely dissolved.

3 Turn up the heat and simmer until the toffee turns an amber colour.

4 Ask an adult to help you remove the pan from the heat. Carefully add the lemon juice – take care as the hot toffee may splutter. Working quickly, dip each apple into the toffee and swirl it around until evenly coated.

5 Leave to cool for 30 seconds, then dip the bottoms of the apples in mixed nuts or sprinkles, if using. Sit the apples on the baking parchment to harden. Serve on the same day.

chocolate truffles

**50 g unsalted butter,
   at room temperature**
**75 g light brown soft
   sugar**
150 ml double cream
175 g dark chocolate

Toppings
**150 g milk or dark
   chocolate, chopped**
chocolate sprinkles
cocoa powder
edible silver balls
**chopped nuts (hazelnuts
   or flaked almonds)**

*a baking tray, lined with
   baking parchment*

makes about 20

1 Ask an adult to help you put the butter, sugar and cream in a saucepan over low heat. Leave until it comes to the boil and the sugar has melted.

2 Break the chocolate into small pieces and tip into a heatproof bowl. Carefully pour the melted butter mixture over the chocolate and stir until the chocolate is melted, smooth and shiny. Leave to cool, then cover with clingfilm and chill in the fridge until it's firm.

3 Making one truffle at a time, scoop a teaspoonful of the chocolate mixture and roll quickly between your hands into a ball. Place on the prepared baking tray.

4 For the toppings, **ask an adult to help you** put the chocolate in a heatproof bowl over a pan of simmering water or in the microwave on a low setting. Stir very carefully until it has melted. Leave to cool slightly.

5 Sprinkle each of your chosen toppings onto a separate plate.

6 Scoop a teaspoonful of the melted chocolate into the palm of your hand and roll one truffle at a time into it to coat completely.

7 Roll in one of the toppings. Repeat with the remaining truffles and leave to set on the baking tray before serving or packing into a pretty box.

These truffles make a delicious gift that you can make yourself. Choose between covering them simply with a dusting of cocoa or a variety of nuts and sprinkles.

You will need an adult to help you with this recipe, but it's worth it because it's one that everyone will enjoy eating! Package the fudge into boxes and tie up with fancy ribbons as great gifts.

fudge

125 g unsalted butter

200 ml evaporated milk

450 g caster sugar

1 teaspoon vanilla extract

50 g dark chocolate,
    chopped

40 g raisins

40 g toasted hazelnuts,
    chopped

*2 x 15-cm square tins,
    oiled with sunflower oil*

makes about 50 chunks

1 Put the butter, evaporated milk, sugar, vanilla extract and 50 ml water in a large, heavy-based saucepan. **Ask an adult to help you** put it over low heat and stir constantly until the butter has melted and the sugar dissolved.

2 Increase the heat and bring the mixture to a gentle boil. Cook for about 10 minutes. To test if it is ready, **ask an adult to help you** drop half a teaspoon of the hot fudge into a cup of cold water and if it forms a soft ball, it is ready.

3 **Ask an adult to help you** remove the pan from the heat and, working quickly, divide the fudge between 2 bowls.

4 Drop the chocolate into one of the bowls, allow to melt into the fudge and stir gently until smooth. Add half the raisins and hazelnuts, stir and quickly pour into one tin. Smooth the top with a knife and leave to set.

5 Beat the vanilla fudge with a wooden spoon until it thickens slightly, add the remaining raisins and hazelnuts, stir and pour into the second tin. Smooth the top with a knife and leave to set.

6 When the fudge is cold, turn it out of the tins onto a board and cut into chunks to serve.

cranberry & pear relish

300 g fresh cranberries
200 g golden caster sugar
1 cinnamon stick
1 teaspoon ground ginger
grated zest and freshly
  squeezed juice of
  1 orange
4 ripe pears

3 small sterilized jars
  (see page 4)

makes about 3 jars

1 Put the cranberries, 150 ml water, the sugar, cinnamon stick, ground ginger and orange zest and juice into a large saucepan. **Ask an adult to help you** put it over medium heat. Cook until the cranberries have softened and burst, then simmer for another 5 minutes.

2 Peel the pears, cut into quarters and remove the cores. Chop the pears into small pieces and add to the pan.

3 Cook for a further 15–20 minutes until the pears are soft and the sauce has thickened.

4 Ask an adult to help you remove the pan from the heat. Carefully fish out the cinnamon stick. Taste the sauce and add a little more sugar if needed.

5 Spoon the relish into the sterilized jars, leave to cool, then cover with the sterilized lids. Store in the fridge until needed.

This is the perfect Christmas relish, as it goes well with baked ham or roast turkey. Why not tie the jars up with labels and ribbons and give away as gifts? Keep the relish in the fridge for up to 2 weeks.

These little nutty cookies look like silvery moons with their dusting of icing sugar. This recipe uses almonds, but you could use chopped mixed nuts instead – simply grind them in the food processor before adding to the mixture. Look out for the bags of ready-chopped mixed nuts in the baking section of the supermarket.

almond crescents

**100 g icing sugar, plus
extra for dusting**

**200 g unsalted butter,
softened**

1 egg yolk

1 teaspoon vanilla extract

300 g plain flour

1 teaspoon baking powder

**100 g ground almonds,
hazelnuts or mixed nuts**

*2 baking trays, lined with
baking parchment*

makes about 24

1 Put the icing sugar, butter, egg yolk and vanilla extract in the bowl of an electric mixer (or use a large bowl and an electric whisk). **Ask an adult to help you** cream the ingredients until smooth and light.

2 Add the flour, baking powder and ground nuts and mix until the dough comes together into a ball. Flatten into a disc, cover with clingfilm and chill in the fridge for 1 hour, or until firm.

3 Preheat the oven to 180°C (350°F) Gas 4.

4 Break off a walnut-sized piece of the cookie dough and roll into a short, fat sausage shape in your hands. Bend into a crescent and place on one of the prepared baking trays.

5 Repeat with the remaining dough, spacing the cookies well apart on the trays.

6 Ask an adult to help you put the trays on the middle shelf of the preheated oven. Bake for about 12 minutes or until golden.

7 Ask an adult to help you remove the trays from the oven. Leave to cool for 2 minutes, then dust with plenty of icing sugar. Leave to cool completely before serving.

iced Christmas tree cookies

225 g unsalted butter,
   softened
225 g caster sugar
1 egg, lightly beaten
½ teaspoon vanilla extract
a pinch of salt
450 g plain flour
Glacé Icing (page 8)
assorted coloured writing
   icing tubes
sugar balls and edible
   sprinkles

*assorted Christmas tree
   cookie cutters*

*2 solid baking trays, lined
   with baking parchment*

*makes 12–16, depending
on size*

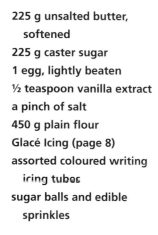

1 Put the butter and sugar in the bowl of an electric mixer fitted with the paddle attachment (or use a large bowl and an electric whisk). **Ask an adult to help you** cream them until pale and fluffy. Add the beaten egg, vanilla extract and salt and mix again.

2 Gradually add the flour and mix until incorporated and smooth. Tip the dough out onto the work surface, flatten into a disc, cover with clingfilm and chill for a couple of hours until firm.

3 Sprinkle a little flour on a clean work surface. Using a rolling pin, roll out the dough to a thickness of about 3–4 mm. Stamp out shapes with the cookie cutters and arrange on the prepared baking trays. Gather up any scraps of cookie dough, knead very lightly to bring together into a ball and roll out again to stamp out more cookies. Chill in the fridge for a further 15 minutes.

4 Preheat the oven to 180°C (350°F) Gas 4.

5 **Ask an adult to help you** put the baking trays on the middle shelf of the preheated oven. Bake for about 10–12 minutes until pale golden and firm to the touch.

6 **Ask an adult to help you** remove the trays from the oven. Leave the cookies to cool on the baking trays before transferring to a wire rack to cool completely.

7 When the cookies are cold, use a small palette knife to carefully spread the Glacé Icing over each cookie, trying to keep it as neat as possible. Use the writing icing tubes to pipe tinsel across each cookie. Position the sugar balls and edible sprinkles over the top to look like tree ornaments.

8 Leave the icing to set before serving.

Treat these simple
Christmas tree cookies
like your own blank
canvas to draw any
decorative design
that you like. Look
for colourful edible
sprinkles and writing
icing pens at the
supermarket to help
you embellish them.

41

This is a popular Christmas biscuit that can either be made the traditional way — in a circle — and cut into wedges, or in a rectangle and then cut into fingers. You could always flavour the basic shortbread dough with lemon zest or even some stem ginger, if you like.

shortbread

175 g plain flour

25 g rice flour, fine semolina or cornflour

75 g caster sugar, plus extra for sprinkling

a pinch of salt

175 g unsalted butter, chilled and diced

a baking tray, lined with baking parchment

makes 8 wedges

1 Sift the flour, rice flour, sugar and salt into a large mixing bowl. Add the chilled butter and rub in with your fingertips until you get a ball of dough.

2 Sprinkle a little flour on a clean work surface. Tip the dough out of the bowl and onto the work surface. Press or roll the dough into a circle about 20 cm across. Alternatively, you can flatten the dough into a rough rectangle.

3 Carefully lift the shortbread dough onto the middle of the prepared baking tray.

4 Working your way around the edge of the circle, press the dough between your thumb and forefinger to create a crinkled border.

5 Using a knife, mark 8 wedges into the shortbread, but don't cut all the way through.

6 Chill the shortbread dough in the fridge for 30 minutes.

7 Preheat the oven to 150°C (300°F) Gas 2.

8 Prick the shortbread all over with a fork and sprinkle with more caster sugar. **Ask an adult to help you** put the baking tray on the middle shelf of the preheated oven. Bake for about 45–50 minutes until light golden.

9 Ask an adult to help you remove the tray from the oven. Leave the shortbread to cool a little before cutting into wedges, following the marks you made before baking.

*Serve these scrummy squares with a good
scoop of the very best vanilla ice cream or
pop into your lunchbox for a special treat.*

pecan, toffee & chocolate squares

125 g plain flour
50 g icing sugar
125 g unsalted butter,
  chilled and diced
1 egg white

Topping
40 g unsalted butter
150 g light muscovado
  sugar
3 eggs
1 teaspoon vanilla extract
200 ml maple syrup
100 g dark chocolate chips
200 g pecan pieces

a 20-cm square baking tin
  (4 cm deep), greased

makes 16

1 Preheat the oven to 180°C (350°F) Gas 4.

2 Ask an adult to help you put the flour, sugar and butter into a food processor. Using the pulse button, process until the mixture just starts to come together in clumps. Tip the mixture into the prepared baking tin and pat evenly over the bottom of the tin.

3 Ask an adult to help you put the baking tin on the middle shelf of the preheated oven. Bake for 20 minutes, or until lightly golden.

4 Ask an adult to help you remove the tin from the oven. Using a pastry brush, very carefully brush the top of the shortbread with the egg white and return to the oven for a further 2 minutes.

5 Ask an adult to help you remove the tin from the oven and leave it to cool while you prepare the topping. Keep the oven on.

6 To make the topping, **ask an adult to help you** melt the butter in a small saucepan over low heat or in the microwave on a low setting.

7 In a small mixing bowl, whisk together the sugar, eggs, vanilla extract, maple syrup and melted butter with a balloon whisk.

8 Scatter the chocolate chips and pecans evenly over the cooled shortbread base. Pour the filling on top. **Ask an adult to help you** put the baking tin on the middle shelf of the preheated oven. Bake for a further 35 minutes, or until the topping has set.

9 Ask an adult to help you remove the tin from the oven and leave it to cool completely in the tin before cutting into squares to serve.

44

You could add some finely grated lemon zest or lemon extract in place of the vanilla if you prefer in these little French cakes. You do need a special madeleine tray for this recipe — there really is no other way to cook these delicate treats.

madeleines

110 g unsalted butter

100 g caster sugar

2 eggs

1 teaspoon vanilla extract

100 g plain flour, plus
  extra for dusting

½ teaspoon baking
  powder

a pinch of salt

a madeleine tray

makes about 24

1 Preheat the oven to 190°C (375°F) Gas 5.

2 Ask an adult to help you melt the butter in a saucepan over low heat or in the microwave on a low setting. Use some of the melted butter to brush the holes in the madeleine tin so that they are lightly greased. Dust the holes with flour and shake off any excess.

3 Put the sugar and eggs in the bowl of an electric mixer fitted with the whisk attachment (or use a large bowl and an electric whisk). **Ask an adult to help you** whisk on medium speed until the mixture has doubled in volume and is very pale and light.

4 Add the vanilla extract. Sift the flour, baking powder and salt into the bowl and fold gently into the egg mixture using a large metal spoon.

5 Fold in the remaining melted butter.

6 Spoon the mixture into the holes in the madeleine tin, filling them to just below the tops. You may need to bake the madeleines in 2 batches if your tin isn't big enough.

7 Ask an adult to help you put the tin on the middle shelf of the preheated oven. Bake for about 10 minutes or until golden brown and well risen.

8 Ask an adult to help you remove the tin from the oven. Leave to cool in the tin for a minute, then turn the tin upside down and tap on the work surface so that the madeleines drop out. Leave to cool completely on a wire rack, then dust with icing sugar, if you like.

Biscotti are a traditional Italian biscuit and are very easy to make. The word 'biscotti' means 'twice baked'. These are made with pistachios and dried cranberries, but you could also use dried figs, raisins and other nuts, such as almonds or hazelnuts. They are delicious with a glass of cold milk.

biscotti with pistachios & cranberries

50 g unsalted butter

225 g plain flour

150 g caster sugar

a pinch of salt

½ teaspoon baking
   powder

75 g shelled pistachios,
   roughly chopped

75 g dried cranberries

grated zest of ½ lemon

1 whole egg

1 yolk

1 teaspoon vanilla extract

2 baking trays

makes about 20

1 Preheat the oven to 180°C (350°F) Gas 4 and line one baking tray with baking parchment.

2 Ask an adult to help you melt the butter in a small saucepan over low heat or in the microwave on a low setting.

3 Tip the flour, sugar, salt and baking powder into a large mixing bowl. Add the pistachios, dried cranberries and grated lemon zest and mix well with a wooden spoon.

4 In a separate small bowl, whisk together the whole egg, egg yolk, vanilla extract and melted butter with a balloon whisk.

5 Make a hole like a well in the middle of the large bowl of dry ingredients and pour the egg and butter mixture into it. Stir with a wooden spoon until the ingredients are thoroughly mixed and have come together into a ball. Divide the dough into 2 equal pieces.

6 Sprinkle a little flour on a clean work surface. Using your hands, roll each piece of dough into a fat sausage about 20 cm long. Put the logs on the lined baking tray, leaving plenty of space between them.

7 Ask an adult to help you put the tray on the middle shelf of the preheated oven. Bake for about 35–45 minutes until golden brown and firm to the touch.

8 Ask an adult to help you remove the tray from the oven and leave to cool for about 45 minutes. Turn the oven off.

9 When the logs are cold, preheat the oven to 170°C (325°F) Gas 3 and line 2 baking trays with baking parchment.

10 Ask an adult to help you to slice the logs diagonally into 1-cm thick slices using a long, sharp knife. Spread them on the baking trays.

11 Ask an adult to help you put the trays on the middle shelf of the preheated oven. Bake for about 20 minutes, or until crisp. You may need to swap the trays over and turn the biscotti halfway through cooking. Leave the biscotti to cool before serving.

These are filled with a sugary cinnamon butter and topped with a crazy drizzle of icing. Add chocolate chips to the filling for an extra helping of sweetness!

cinnamon sticky buns

150 ml milk

500–600 g strong
white flour

1 x 7-g sachet easy-blend
dried yeast

a large pinch of salt

50 g caster sugar

2 eggs, lightly beaten

75 g unsalted butter,
softened

Glacé Icing (page 8)

Filling

100 g unsalted butter,
softened

100 g light brown soft
sugar

3 teaspoons ground
cinnamon

75 g pecan pieces

*a 23 x 30-cm baking tin,
greased*

makes 12

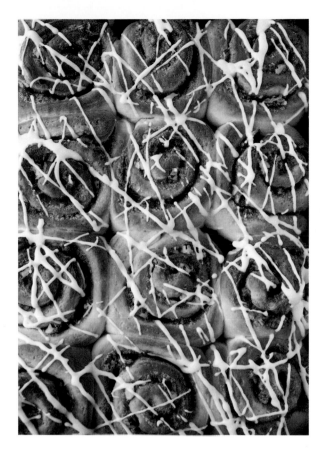

1 Ask an adult to help you heat the milk in a small saucepan until hot but not boiling.

2 Sift 500 g of the flour into a large mixing bowl and stir in the yeast, salt and sugar. Make a hole like a well in the middle and pour in the warm milk, eggs and butter. Stir until mixed.

3 To knead the dough, sprinkle a little flour on a clean work surface. Shape the dough into a ball and push on it and press it onto the work surface, turning it round often. You'll need to keep doing this until it is silky smooth and elastic – about 5 minutes – and you may need to add more flour if the dough is too sticky.

4 Shape the dough into a neat ball again. Wash and dry the mixing bowl and sit the dough back in it. Cover tightly with clingfilm and leave in a warm place until the dough has doubled in size. This will take about 1½ hours.

5 While the dough is rising, make the filling. Put the butter, sugar, cinnamon and pecans in a bowl. Beat with a wooden spoon until mixed.

6 Tip the dough onto the floured work surface and knead lightly for 1 minute. Roll and press it into a rectangle about 30 x 50 cm, with a long side nearest you.

7 Spread the filling over the dough, leaving a border of about 1 cm around the edges.

8 Starting with the side closest to you, roll the dough up evenly and firmly, but not too tight. Cut into 12 slices and place cut-side up in the baking tin. Lightly oil a sheet of clingfilm, then use it to loosely cover the baking tin (oiled-side down). Leave in a warm place for 30 minutes, or until risen.

9 Preheat the oven to 180°C (350°F) Gas 4.

10 Ask an adult to help you put the tin on the middle shelf of the preheated oven. Bake for 30–35 minutes until golden brown.

11 Ask an adult to help you remove the tin from the oven and leave it to cool completely.

12 Using a spoon, drizzle the Glacé Icing over the buns. Leave to set before tipping them out of the tin and pulling them apart, to serve.

rocky road fridge cake

100 g mixed nuts (eg hazelnuts, almonds, pecan nuts, walnuts)

400 g dark chocolate, chopped

50 g unsalted butter

1 rounded tablespoon clear honey

250 g mixed dried fruit (eg glacé cherries, figs, apricots, raisins)

75 g digestive biscuits

a 20-cm square baking tin, lined with baking parchment

makes 16

1 Ask an adult to help you put the nuts in a frying pan over medium heat. Toast the nuts for a couple of minutes, until golden, shaking the pan from time to time so that they don't burn. **Ask an adult to help you** remove the pan from the heat and chop the nuts.

2 Ask an adult to help you put the chocolate, butter and honey in a heatproof bowl over a pan of simmering water or in the microwave on a low setting. Stir very carefully until melted. Leave to cool slightly.

3 Halve the glacé cherries and roughly chop the figs and apricots. Break the biscuits into small pieces.

4 Add the toasted nuts, dried fruit and biscuits to the melted chocolate mixture and stir with a wooden spoon until combined. Spoon into the prepared tin and spread evenly. Leave to cool, then cover lightly with clingfilm and chill in the fridge until set.

5 Cut into 16 squares and serve.

Everyone loves chocolate fridge cake and there is no end to the variety of bits and pieces you can put in it. Choose from your favourite dried fruit and nuts, and maybe add some mini-marshmallows if the mood takes you.

These pretty snowflakes are simply made from a basic meringue, but add a festive touch with a sprinkling of edible silver glitter or silver balls.

meringue snowflakes

150 g caster sugar
75 g egg whites (about
  2 medium egg whites)
edible silver glitter
edible silver balls

a piping bag, fitted with
  a star-shaped nozzle

2 solid baking trays, lined
  with baking parchment

makes about 12

1 Preheat the oven to 200°C (400°F) Gas 6.

2 Tip the sugar into a small roasting tin. **Ask an adult to help you** put it in the preheated oven for about 5 minutes until hot to the touch – be careful not to burn your fingers!

3 Turn the oven down to 110°C (225°F) Gas ¼.

4 Place the egg whites in a large, clean mixing bowl or in the bowl of an electric mixer. **Ask an adult to help you** to beat the egg whites (with an electric whisk, if necessary) until they're frothy.

5 Tip the hot sugar onto the egg whites in one go and continue to whisk on high speed for about 5 minutes until the meringue mixture is very stiff, white and cold.

6 Spoon the meringue mixture into the prepared piping bag. Pipe little blobs of meringue onto the prepared baking trays in the shape of snowflakes. Scatter silver glitter or silver balls over the top.

7 **Ask an adult to help you** put the trays in the preheated oven. Bake for about 45 minutes or until crisp and dry. Turn off the oven, leave the door closed and let the snowflakes cool down completely inside the oven.

uncooked batter for Easy
    Fruit Cake (page 94)
uncooked dough for
    Gingerbread Shooting
    Stars (page 70)
350 g royal icing sugar
green good colouring
    paste
orange food colouring
    paste
4 tablespoons apricot jam
125 g natural marzipan
150 g white ready-to-use
    fondant or royal icing
Christmas sprinkles

*8 mini loaf tins, greased
    and base-lined with
    greased baking
    parchment*

*a carrot-shaped cookie
    cutter*

*a baking tray, lined with
    baking parchment*

a mini star-shaped cutter

makes lots!

goodies for Santa & Rudolf

1 Preheat the oven to 180°C (350°F) Gas 4.

2 Prepare the Easy Fruit Cake as described on page 94. Divide the mixture between the prepared loaf tins, filling them just over two-thirds full. Arrange them on a baking tray and **ask an adult to help you** put it on the middle shelf of the preheated oven. Bake for about 30 minutes, or until golden brown, well risen and a skewer inserted into the middle of the cakes comes out clean.

3 **Ask an adult to help you** remove the tray from the oven and leave the cakes to cool for 10 minutes before tipping them out onto a wire rack to cool completely.

4 Prepare the gingerbread dough as described on page 70 and leave it to rest in the fridge for a couple of hours, or until firm.

5 Sprinkle a little plain flour on a clean work surface. Using a rolling pin, roll out the dough to a thickness of about 3 mm. Stamp out carrot shapes with the cookie cutter and arrange on the prepared baking tray. Gather up any scraps of dough, knead very lightly to bring together into a ball and roll out again to stamp out more cookies.

6 **Ask an adult to help you** put the tray on the middle shelf of the preheated oven. Bake for about 12 minutes, or until firm.

7 Leave the cookies to cool on the baking trays for about 5 minutes before transferring to a wire rack to cool completely.

8 When the cookies are cold, use the royal icing sugar to make up the icing according to the manufacturer's instructions. Tint a quarter of the icing green using the food colouring paste. Tint the remaining icing orange.

9 Ice the cookies to look like carrots using the coloured royal icing and spreading it evenly with a small palette knife. Leave to dry completely before serving.

10 To decorate the cakes, **ask an adult to help you** put the apricot jam in a small saucepan over low heat. Leave until runny, then sieve. Brush the top of each cake with a thin layer of the jam.

11 Lightly dust the work surface with icing sugar and roll out the marzipan until it is no more than 2 mm thick. Using the bottom of a mini loaf tin as a guide, cut out 8 rectangles from the marzipan and lay one rectangle on top of each cake.

12 Repeat step 11 with the fondant icing and stick the rectangles on top of the marzipan with a little boiled water. Use the star-shaped cutter to stamp out stars. Dab the bottom of each star with water and stick onto the top of each cake. Very lightly brush the stars with a little more water and scatter Christmas sprinkles over the top. Set aside to dry.

13 On Christmas Eve, arrange your choice of goodies on a tray, eg a bowl of popcorn, a few sweets, a clementine and a glass of milk.

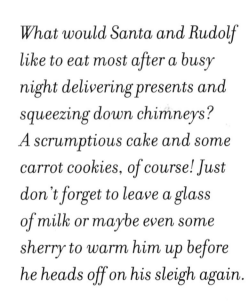

What would Santa and Rudolf like to eat most after a busy night delivering presents and squeezing down chimneys? A scrumptious cake and some carrot cookies, of course! Just don't forget to leave a glass of milk or maybe even some sherry to warm him up before he heads off on his sleigh again.

Topped with a pastry star and filled with cinnamon-spiced apples and cranberries, these little pies are a delicious alternative to mince pies. Use shop-bought sweet pastry to make them in no time at all!

apple & cranberry pies

2 Bramley apples

2 red eating apples

375 g ready-made sweet pastry

50 g caster sugar, plus extra for sprinkling

½ teaspoon ground cinnamon, plus extra for sprinkling

juice of ½ lemon

50 g dried cranberries

1 tablespoon milk

a 12-hole tartlet tin

a fluted round cookie cutter, just bigger than the tartlet tin holes

a star-shaped cutter

makes 9–12

1 Peel both varieties of apple, cut into quarters and remove the cores. Chop the apples into small pieces and tip into a medium saucepan. Add the sugar, cinnamon, lemon juice and cranberries. **Ask an adult to help you** put the pan over low-medium heat, stirring from time to time until the apples are tender.

2 Ask an adult to help you remove the pan from the heat. Taste and add a little more sugar if needed. Set aside until cold.

3 Preheat the oven to 180°C (350°F) Gas 4.

4 Sprinkle a little flour on a clean work surface. Roll out the dough to a thickness of about 2 mm. Use the fluted cookie cutter to stamp out rounds. Gently press the pastry rounds into the tin holes.

5 Divide the cooled fruit mixture between the pies, filling them almost to the top.

6 Gather up any scraps of dough, knead very lightly to bring together into a ball and roll out again. Use the star-shaped cutter to stamp out stars for the pie tops.

7 Lightly brush the edges of each pie with milk and top with a pastry star. Brush the top of each star with milk and dust with caster sugar and a little ground cinnamon.

8 Ask an adult to help you put the tin on the middle shelf of the preheated oven. Bake for about 25 minutes, or until the pastry is golden brown and the fruit filling is bubbling.

9 Ask an adult to help you remove the tin from the oven. Leave to cool, then dust with icing sugar, if you like.

edible decorations

Once you have decided which animal or shape to do, you can colour your marzipan accordingly. Use the figures to decorate the Christmas table or even a cake.

marzipan Christmas figures

**200 g natural marzipan
assorted food colouring
pastes**

makes roughly 10 figures

to make one reindeer

1 Break off 4 walnut-sized pieces of marzipan from the block. Add a bit of red food colouring to one piece of marzipan and knead it until the colour is evenly mixed in. Repeat this process to tint the other pieces yellow and black. Leave the fourth piece white. Cover with clingfilm.

2 Break off another piece of marzipan the size of a satsuma and tint it brown. Break off a piece of this slightly smaller than a walnut and roll into a ball. Break off another piece the size of a cherry tomato and roll into a ball. Stick onto the larger piece, slightly forwards, for the head. Roll 6 small nuggets of brown marzipan into balls. Flatten 2 of them and stick to the top of the head for the ears. Attach the remaining 4 around the body for legs.

3 Roll a small nugget of red marzipan into a ball and attach to the face for the nose.

4 To make the eyes, break off 2 tiny pieces of white marzipan, roll into balls and flatten into discs. Roll 2 smaller balls of black marzipan into discs and stick in the middle of the white discs. Attach the eyes to the reindeer's face.

5 Finally, break off 2 small nuggets of yellow marzipan and shape roughly into antlers. Attach to the top of the head.

to make one snowman

1 Break off a small walnut-sized piece of marzipan from the block and tint it red using the food colouring paste. Take a slightly smaller piece of marzipan and tint it black with the food colouring. Tint another tiny piece orange. Cover with clingfilm.

2 Break off another piece of marzipan the size of a satsuma. Divide this in 2 – one piece slightly larger than the other. Roll both into balls and put the larger one on the work surface for the body. Stick the smaller ball on top for the head.

3 Roll the red marzipan into a thin snake and wrap this carefully around the snowman's neck for a scarf.

4 To make the eyes and buttons, break off 4 tiny pieces of black marzipan. Roll into balls and stick 2 of each onto the face and body.

5 Roll the orange marzipan into a carrot shape for the nose. Stick this in the middle of the snowman's face.

to make one penguin

1 Break off a tiny piece of marzipan and tint it orange using the food colouring paste. Break off a satsuma-sized piece of marzipan from the block and tint it black. Break off a walnut-sized piece and leave it white. Cover with clingfilm.

2 Break off a cherry tomato-sized piece of black marzipan and roll into a ball for the penguin's head.

3 Reserve a tiny amount of white marzipan for the eyes. Roll the rest into a ball and put on the work surface for the body. Stick the black ball on top for the head.

4 Take a piece of the remaining black marzipan and flatten into a disc about the same width as the penguin's body and stick it onto the back of the penguin.

5 Take 2 smaller pieces of black marzipan and shape into wing shapes. Attach to the side of the body.

6 For the feet, take 2 small nuggets of black marzipan, roll into balls and flatten into oval discs. Press onto the bottom of the penguin's body so that they are clearly visible.

7 To make the eyes, take the reserved white marzipan, roll into 2 tiny balls and flatten into discs. Roll 2 smaller balls of black marzipan into discs and stick in the middle of the white discs. Attach the eyes to the penguin's face.

8 Roll and pinch the orange marzipan into a beak shape. Stick this onto the penguin's face.

Make these little mice at least one day before you want to serve them to give them plenty of time to dry out. The recipe makes enough for a large family of mice — one for each of your family and friends.

sugar mice

1 egg white
1 teaspoon lemon juice
400–500 g icing sugar,
   sifted
pink food colouring paste
small chocolate sprinkles

kitchen string

a baking tray, lined with
   baking parchment

makes 12

1 Put the egg white in a large bowl and whisk with a balloon whisk until foamy. Stir in the lemon juice.

2 Gradually add the icing sugar and stir in with a wooden spoon until really stiff, like dough. It might be easier to dust the work surface with icing sugar and knead the sugar into the mixture until you get the right consistency.

3 Divide the mixture in 2. Add a tiny bit of pink food colouring to one half and knead it until all the colour is evenly mixed in. Add a tiny bit more colouring if you want a stronger colour.

4 Break off walnut-sized pieces of mixture and roll into a cone shape. Pinch little ears on top of the narrow end. Squeeze the narrow end into a nose. Press a chocolate sprinkle into the face below the ears to make the eyes. Cut a length of string about 3–4 cm and push it into the round end of the mouse to make the tail.

5 Use a wooden skewer to dab a tiny amount of pink food colouring on the nose. Put the mouse on the prepared baking tray.

6 Repeat with the remaining mixture and leave the mice to dry out for at least 12 hours.

65

Advent numbered cookies

Vanilla shortbread

225 g unsalted butter, softened

250 g plain flour

½ teaspoon salt

75 g icing sugar, sifted

1 teaspoon vanilla extract

Chocolate shortbread

225 g unsalted butter, softened

200 g plain flour

50 g cocoa powder

½ teaspoon salt

75 g icing sugar, sifted

1 teaspoon vanilla extract

assorted cookie cutters, eg round, square and oval

numbered cookie cutters

1–2 solid baking trays, lined with baking parchment

24 cellophane bags

makes about 24

1 To make the vanilla shortbread, beat the butter in a mixing bowl with a wooden spoon until smooth and very soft. Meanwhile, sift together the flour and salt.

2 Add the icing sugar to the creamed butter and continue mixing until light and fluffy. Add the vanilla and mix again. Add the sifted flour and salt and mix until it starts to come together into a dough.

3 To knead the dough, first sprinkle a little flour on a clean work surface. Then shape the dough into a ball and push on it and press it onto the work surface, turning it round often. Do this for a minute, then flatten into a disc, cover with clingfilm and chill until needed.

4 To make the chocolate shortbread, follow steps 1–3 above, but add the cocoa powder to the flour and salt.

5 Preheat the oven to 180°C (350°F) Gas 4.

6 Sprinkle more flour on the work surface. Using a rolling pin, roll out the vanilla and chocolate dough (separately) to a thickness of 2–3 mm and stamp out 24 shapes using the assorted cookie cutters. Arrange on the prepared baking trays. Using the numbered cutters, stamp out numbers 1–24 and stick to each larger cookie with a dab of cold water.

7 Leave the cookies to chill in the fridge for 10 minutes.

8 **Ask an adult to help you** put one tray on the middle shelf of the preheated oven. Bake for about 12 minutes, or until firm and starting to go crisp at the edges. Repeat with the second tray of cookies.

9 **Ask an adult to help you** remove the cookies from the oven and leave to cool on the trays before packaging into cellophane bags, if you like.

You will need a selection of numbered cookie cutters, preferably in different sizes, and plain cutters in different shapes to make these. Give them away to friends and family to celebrate Advent.

This is a very simple, edible Christmas decoration. Why not add some of your favourite sweets to the garlands too?

popcorn garlands

sunflower oil, for frying
popcorn kernels

*needle and assorted
brightly coloured
threads*

1 Put 1 tablespoon of oil in a large saucepan. **Ask an adult to help you** put it over medium-high heat. Add enough popcorn to cover the base of the pan, cover tightly with a lid and wait for the popping to start.

2 Holding the pan and lid firmly with oven gloves, give the pan a good shake from time to time.

3 When the popping stops, then all the kernels have popped and you can safely take off the lid and remove the pan from the heat. Tip the popcorn into a large bowl and leave to cool.

4 Thread the needle with a long piece of the coloured thread and tie a big, double knot at the end. One by one, push a piece of popcorn onto the thread until you have a long garland. Repeat using different-coloured threads.

5 Arrange the popcorn garlands on the Christmas tree or anywhere that you might need some edible decorations!

While you've got some popcorn on the go, why not make these perfect party nibbles?! They take just moments to make.

popcorn marshmallow clusters

1 tablespoon unsalted
   butter
125 g mini-marshmallows
75–100 g popped popcorn
75 g pecan pieces
75 g dried cranberries
edible silver balls

*a baking tray, lined with
   baking parchment*

makes loads!

1 Put the butter in a large saucepan. **Ask an adult to help you** put it over medium heat. Add the marshmallows and give them a good stir. Once they start to melt, add the popcorn, pecans and cranberries. Stir constantly until the marshmallows melt and the mixture starts to clump together.

2 Carefully tip the mixture out of the pan and onto the prepared baking tray. Scatter over some edible silver balls.

3 Once the mixture is cool enough to handle, break off clusters and serve in baskets or piled up on plates.

If you've ever been lucky enough to see a real shooting star, you'll no doubt have closed your eyes and made a wish. Ice these cute cookies in elaborate patterns and scatter with edible silver or gold balls so that they look as if they would shine brightly if they raced across the night sky.

gingerbread shooting stars

375 g plain flour

½ teaspoon baking powder

1 teaspoon bicarbonate
    of soda

3 teaspoons ground ginger

½ teaspoon ground
    cinnamon

a pinch of salt

125 g unsalted butter,
    softened

75 g dark muscovado sugar

1 egg, lightly beaten

100 ml golden syrup

Glacé Icing (page 8)

edible silver balls

*assorted shooting star-
    shaped cookie cutters*

*2 baking trays, lined with
    baking parchment*

makes about 24

1 Sift together the flour, baking powder, bicarbonate of soda, ginger, cinnamon and salt in a mixing bowl.

2 Ask an adult to help you cream the butter and sugar together in the bowl of an electric mixer (or use a large bowl and an electric whisk). Add the beaten egg and golden syrup and mix until smooth. Add the sifted dry ingredients and mix again until smooth.

3 To knead the dough, first sprinkle a little flour on a clean work surface. Then shape the dough into a ball and push on it and press it onto the work surface, turning it round often. Do this for a minute, then flatten into a disc, cover with clingfilm and chill for a couple of hours until firm.

4 Preheat the oven to 180°C (350°F) Gas 4.

5 Sprinkle more flour on the work surface. Using a rolling pin, roll out the dough to a thickness of about 5 mm. Stamp out shapes with the cookie cutters and arrange on the prepared baking trays. Gather up any scraps of cookie dough, knead very lightly to bring together into a ball and roll out again to stamp out more cookies. **Ask an adult to help you** put the trays on the middle shelf of the preheated oven. Bake for about 10 minutes.

6 Ask an adult to help you remove the cookies from the oven and leave to cool on the trays for a couple of minutes before transferring to a wire rack to cool completely.

7 Make a piping bag as described on page 16. Pipe Glacé Icing onto the cookies and decorate with silver balls. Leave on a wire rack to dry.

There's no cooking required for this edible, decorative idea, but it's an easy and fun way for small hands to get involved in the festive fun.

candy trees

assorted festive sweets

roll of clear cellophane or cellophane bags

brightly coloured ribbons

silver spray-painted branches and twigs

1 Tip all the sweets into a large bowl and mix them up!

2 Ask an adult to help you cut large squares from the cellophane. You don't need to do this if you have cellophane bags already. Arrange a handful of sweets in the middle of each square. Gather up the cellophane to make a pouch and tie with pretty festive ribbons, leaving enough ribbon to make a loop.

3 Arrange the silver branches and twigs in a sturdy vase. Hang the parcels on the tree.

I always used to make frosted fruit when I was little and it was piled high on a glass serving dish and given pride of place on the dinner table. Use a selection of green and red grapes, blueberries and cranberries. In the summer months you could try frosting strands of jewel-like redcurrants.

frosted fruit

1 egg white
1 bunch of green
   grapes
1 bunch of red grapes
a handful of
   cranberries
a handful of
   blueberries

caster sugar, for
   sprinkling

*a baking tray, lined
   with baking
   parchment*

makes a big plateful

1 Put the egg white in a large bowl and whisk with a balloon whisk until foamy. Using a pastry brush, brush the egg white over the fruit – try to cover them evenly and completely.

2 Hold the bunch of grapes above the prepared baking tray and sprinkle caster sugar over the grapes so that you cover the egg white completely.

3 Lightly brush the cranberries and blueberries with egg white and coat these in sugar too.

4 Leave the fruit to dry on the parchment for at least a couple of hours until the sugar has hardened and become crisp.

5 Arrange the fruit on a platter.

No two snowflakes are the same and these snowflake cookies are no exception. Look out for sets of fancy snowflake cookie cutters in all shapes and sizes and little pots of sparkly edible sprinkles to decorate your cookies with.

snowflake cookies

225 g unsalted butter,
  softened
225 g caster sugar
1 egg, lightly beaten
½ teaspoon vanilla extract
a pinch of salt
450 g plain flour
Glacé Icing (page 8)
edible white glitter
edible silver balls

*assorted snowflake-
  shaped cookie cutters*

*2 baking trays, lined with
  baking parchment*

*makes about 12,
depending on size*

1 Put the butter and sugar in the bowl of an electric mixer fitted with the paddle attachment (or use a large bowl and an electric whisk). **Ask an adult to help you** cream them until pale and fluffy. Add the beaten egg, vanilla extract and salt and mix again.

2 Gradually add the flour and mix until incorporated and smooth. Tip the dough out onto the work surface, flatten into a disc, cover with clingfilm and chill for a couple of hours until firm.

3 Sprinkle a little flour on a clean work surface. Roll out the dough to a thickness of about 5 mm. Stamp out shapes with the cookie cutters and arrange on the prepared baking trays. Gather up any scraps of cookie dough,

knead very lightly to bring together into a ball and roll out again to stamp out more cookies. Chill in the fridge for a further 15 minutes.

4 Preheat the oven to 180°C (350°F) Gas 4.

5 Ask an adult to help you put the baking trays on the middle shelf of the preheated oven. Bake for about 10–12 minutes until pale golden and firm to the touch.

6 Ask an adult to help you remove the trays from the oven. Leave the cookies to cool on the baking trays before transferring to a wire rack to cool completely.

7 Make a piping bag as described on page 16. Pipe Glacé Icing onto the cookies and dust with glitter. Decorate with silver balls.

cakes & desserts

This is a chocolate sponge baked in a tray, and then rolled up and decorated to look like a wooden log. This is traditionally what French people eat for dessert on Christmas Eve. Try it and see if you like it!

bûche de Noël

125 g self-raising flour

3 tablespoons cocoa powder

4 eggs

150 g caster sugar

Chocolate Frosting (page 9)

icing sugar, for dusting

Chocolate bark

150 g chocolate (milk or dark)

a 35 x 25-cm Swiss roll tin, greased and lined with greased baking parchment

a large sheet of baking parchment, sprinkled with caster sugar

2 robins, to decorate (optional)

serves 8

1 Preheat the oven to 190°C (375°F) Gas 5.

2 Dust the prepared Swiss roll tin with a little flour. Tip out the excess flour.

3 Sift the self-raising flour and cocoa together onto a piece of baking parchment.

4 Break the eggs in the bowl of an electric mixer (or use a large bowl and an electric whisk). Add the sugar and **ask an adult to help you** mix on medium-high speed for about 5 minutes until the mixture is very light, pale and foamy, and has doubled in size.

5 Gently tip the flour and cocoa mixture into the bowl and fold in using a large metal spoon. Carefully tip the mixture into the prepared tin and spread it right to the edges, being careful not to knock out too much air.

6 Ask an adult to help you put the tin on the middle shelf of the preheated oven. Bake for 9–10 minutes until the cake bounces back when lightly pressed with your finger. Be careful not to burn your finger!

7 Ask an adult to help you remove the tin from the oven. Using oven gloves, tip the warm sponge out of the tin and upside down onto the prepared sheet of baking parchment.

With one of the long sides nearest you, carefully peel off the parchment. Roll up the sponge with the sugar-dusted paper rolled inside the sponge. Set aside to cool.

8 Make up the Chocolate Frosting as described on page 9. You may need to leave it somewhere cool for 30 minutes to thicken enough to spread.

9 Unroll the sponge and spread the surface with one-third of the frosting. Carefully roll the log back up completely, without the paper this time. Slice one-third off the end at an angle. Arrange the larger piece on a serving plate with the join underneath. Position the smaller third at an angle on one side. Spread the remaining frosting over the cake to cover it.

10 To make the bark, **ask an adult to help you** put the chocolate in a heatproof bowl over a pan of simmering water or in the microwave on a low setting. Stir very carefully until melted.

11 Spread the melted chocolate in a thin layer on a sheet of baking parchment. Leave to set, then break into pieces. Stick the bark onto the log and dust with icing sugar. Decorate with robins, if you like.

This is a delicious French gingerbread cake. Make it a couple of days before you want to eat it so that the flavours of all the spices mixed with the honey will taste much better. Serve it in slices on its own or with a lick of butter.

pain d'épices

225 g plain flour

2 teaspoons baking powder

1 teaspoon ground cinnamon

3 teaspoons ground ginger

¼ teaspoon ground allspice

¼ teaspoon ground cloves

¼ teaspoon salt

150 g unsalted butter, softened

75 g light brown soft sugar

125 ml clear honey

2 eggs, lightly beaten

3–4 tablespoons milk

a 2-lb. loaf tin, greased

makes 10 slices

1 Preheat the oven to 180°C (350°F) Gas 4. Base-line the prepared loaf tin with greased baking parchment.

2 Sift the flour, baking powder, cinnamon, ginger, allspice, cloves and salt together into a mixing bowl and set aside.

3 Put the butter and sugar in the bowl of an electric mixer (or use a large bowl and an electric whisk). **Ask an adult to help you** cream them until pale and light.

4 Add the honey and mix again. Gradually add the beaten eggs, mixing well between each addition and scraping down the bowl with a rubber spatula from time to time.

5 Add the sifted dry ingredients and the milk and mix again until smooth. Spoon into the prepared tin and spread evenly with a knife.

6 Ask an adult to help you put the tin on the middle shelf of the preheated oven. Bake for about 1 hour, or until well risen and a skewer inserted into the middle of the cake comes out clean. You may need to cover the cake loosely with a sheet of foil if it is browning too quickly.

7 Ask an adult to help you remove the cake from the oven. Leave it to cool in the tin for 5 minutes before tipping out onto a wire rack to cool completely.

83

Nothing says Christmas like a gingerbread house and this one is straight out of a fairy tale. You could decorate the cake with any number and type of sweets, so let your imagination run wild. Be aware that you will need to make up the recipe twice.

gingerbread house

Make up this recipe twice

375 g plain flour

½ teaspoon baking powder

1 teaspoon bicarbonate of soda

3 teaspoons ground ginger

½ teaspoon ground cinnamon

¼ teaspoon each of ground cloves and allspice

a pinch of salt

125 g unsalted butter, softened

75 g dark muscovado sugar

1 egg, lightly beaten

100 ml golden syrup

350–500 g royal icing sugar

assorted sweets

3 solid baking trays, lined with baking parchment

a piping bag, fitted with a plain nozzle

serves 12

1 Sift the flour, baking powder, bicarbonate of soda, ginger, cinnamon, cloves, allspice and salt together into a mixing bowl and set aside.

2 Put the butter and muscovado sugar in the bowl of an electric mixer (or use a large bowl and an electric whisk). **Ask an adult to help you** cream them until fluffy.

3 Add the beaten egg and golden syrup and mix until smooth. Add the sifted dry ingredients and mix again until smooth.

4 Sprinkle a little flour on a clean work surface. Shape the dough into a ball and push on it and press it onto the work surface, turning it round often. Do this for a minute, then flatten into a disc, cover with clingfilm and chill for a couple of hours until firm.

5 Repeat steps 1–4 to make a second quantity of gingerbread dough.

6 When you are ready to bake the house, preheat the oven to 180°C (350°F) Gas 4.

7 You will need to make paper templates for the walls and roof of your house. Take a large sheet of paper and draw a rectangle measuring 20 x 11 cm for the roof. Make another paper rectangle measuring 19 x 10 cm for the front and back walls. You will also need a template for the sides – this will be a 10-cm square with a 4-cm high triangle on top.

8 Sprinkle more flour on the work surface. Using a rolling pin, roll out the dough to a thickness of about 3–4 mm. Use your paper templates to cut out 2 roof shapes, 2 big walls and 2 sides. You may find it easier to write on the baking parchment which shapes are which as you cut them out. Arrange them on the prepared baking trays. Carefully cut out windows from the walls and sides.

9 Gather up any scraps of dough, knead very lightly to bring together into a ball and roll out again to stamp out any other cookie shapes that you like. Why not make the carrots for Santa and Rudolf's tray (see page 56)?

10 Ask an adult to help you put the trays on the middle shelf of the preheated oven. You will need to bake the gingerbread in

batches. Bake for about 10–15 minutes until firm and just starting to brown at the edges.

11 Ask an adult to help you remove the gingerbread from the oven and leave to cool completely.

12 Use the royal icing sugar to make icing according to the manufacturer's instructions. It will need to be thick enough to hold its shape when piped, so add the water gradually until you have the correct consistency. Fill the piping bag with the icing. You will need 2 pairs of hands for the next step!

13 Take one gingerbread side and pipe a line of icing along the bottom and up one side (just up to but not including the gables). Hold it up on a serving tray or platter. Take a big wall and pipe some icing along the bottom and 2 sides. Hold this at a right angle to the first, iced side. Pick up the second big wall

and pipe some icing along the bottom and 2 sides. Hold this in place opposite the other wall and so that it meets the side at a right angle. Repeat with the remaining side. You may find it easier to position tins or jars inside the house to hold the walls in place until the icing has set firm.

14 Once the walls are completely set and secure, you can attach the roof. Pipe a line of icing down the gables and position one roof panel on either side of the gables. Pipe a line of icing across the top of the roof. Hold the roof in place until the icing feels firm.

15 To decorate the house, pipe royal-icing patterns onto the roof panels and decorate with your choice of sweets. Pipe borders around the windows and doors, as well as along the bottom of the house, and decorate with sweets as you like.

mini baked Alaskas

**4 x 1-cm thick slices of
    shop-bought chocolate
    loaf cake
2 tablespoons jam or
    chocolate spread
4 scoops of good-quality
    vanilla ice cream
2 egg whites
125 g caster sugar**

a 6-cm round cookie cutter

*a baking tray, lined with
    baking parchment*

makes 4

1 Preheat the oven to 240°C (475°F) Gas 9.

2 Using the cookie cutter, stamp out a round from each slice of chocolate cake and place on the prepared baking tray. Spread ½ tablespoon jam over each round, top with a scoop of ice cream and freeze.

3 Place the egg whites in a large, clean mixing bowl with the salt. **Ask an adult to help you** use an electric whisk to beat the egg whites until they're nice and thick. When you turn the whisk off and lift them up slowly, the egg whites should stand in stiff peaks.

4 Gradually add the sugar, beating well after each addition, then whisk for a further minute until the meringue is very stiff and glossy.

5 Using a palette knife, cover each ball of ice cream and cake with meringue. **Ask an adult to help you** put the tray on the middle shelf of the preheated oven. Bake for 2–3 minutes, or until the meringue begins to turn golden at the edges. Serve immediately.

Who doesn't like ice cream and meringue? Put the two together and you've got the perfect pudding. You could use whichever flavour of ice cream you like. Start these puds in advance, keep in the freezer for a couple of hours and simply bake in the oven when you're ready.

Look out for sparkling cranberry or pomegranate drinks to make these party jellies. Whisking the jelly just before it sets traps the bubbles in the jelly, which gives them some extra 'fizz'.

fruity jellies

8 leaves of gelatine

750 ml either sparkling grape, raspberry or cranberry juice, or pomegranate lemonade

3–4 tablespoons caster sugar, or to taste

1 pomegranate, seeds scooped out

100 g seedless red grapes, halved

100 g blueberries

serves 6–8

1 Soak the gelatine leaves in a bowl of cold water for 5 minutes.

2 Put 250 ml of the juice and the sugar in a saucepan. **Ask an adult to help you** put it over medium heat and heat until just below boiling point.

3 Drain the gelatine leaves, add to the hot juice and stir well until the gelatine is thoroughly dissolved.

4 Pour the remaining juice into a large bowl, add the hot juice and gelatine mixture and mix well with a whisk to combine. Chill in the fridge until starting to set.

5 Meanwhile, set aside about 5 tablespoons of the pomegranate seeds. Mix together the remaining pomegranate seeds, the grapes and blueberries.

6 Once the jelly has started to set, you need to make it bubbly. Quickly whisk the jelly with a balloon whisk to make air bubbles. Fold in the fruit and divide between 6–8 small glasses.

7 Cover with clingfilm and chill in the fridge until completely set.

8 Top the jellies with the reserved pomegranate seeds, to decorate.

Cover this cake with mountains of snowy frosting and a scattering of coconut chips. You'll need a sugar thermometer to make the frosting, and once it is made, you have to work quickly, as it sets fast!

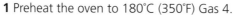

coconut cake

200 g unsalted butter, softened

200 g caster sugar

4 eggs, lightly beaten

1 teaspoon vanilla extract

150 g plain flour

4 teaspoons baking powder

a pinch of salt

75 g desiccated coconut

3 tablespoons soured cream or coconut cream, at room temperature

250 g coconut chips

Marshmallow frosting

175 g caster sugar

3 egg whites

2 x 20-cm round cake tins, greased and base-lined with greased baking parchment

a sugar thermometer

serves 8–10

1 Preheat the oven to 180°C (350°F) Gas 4.

2 Put the butter and sugar in the bowl of an electric mixer (or use a large bowl and an electric whisk). **Ask an adult to help you** cream them until pale and light.

3 Gradually add the beaten eggs, mixing well between each addition and scraping down the side of the bowl with a rubber spatula from time to time. Add the vanilla extract and mix.

4 Sift the flour, baking powder and salt into the bowl and add the desiccated coconut. Fold the dry ingredients into the cake mixture until just mixed using a large metal spoon or rubber spatula. Add the soured cream and mix again until smooth.

5 Divide the mixture between the prepared cake tins. **Ask an adult to help you** put the tins on the middle shelf of the preheated oven. Bake for 20–25 minutes until golden and a skewer inserted into the middle of the cakes comes out clean.

6 **Ask an adult to help you** remove the tins from the oven. Leave to cool for 5 minutes before tipping the cakes out onto a wire rack.

7 To make the Marshmallow Frosting, **ask an adult to help you**. Put the sugar, egg whites and 2 teaspoons water into a large heatproof bowl. Set the bowl over a pan of simmering water – the bottom of the bowl should not touch the water. Whisk slowly with a balloon whisk to dissolve the sugar. Continue cooking and whisking until the mixture reaches 60°C (140°F) on a sugar thermometer. The meringue should double in volume and be hot to touch.

8 Transfer the mixture to a free-standing electric mixer fitted with the whisk attachment (or keep it in the same bowl and use an electric whisk). Continue to whisk on medium speed until the meringue is stiff and very glossy. The frosting is now ready to use straightaway.

9 Place one cake on a serving plate and spread 3–4 rounded tablespoons of the frosting on top. Top with the second cake layer. Working quickly with a palette knife, cover the top and sides of the cake with the meringue frosting, fluffing the frosting into peaks as you do so.

10 Scatter the coconut chips all over the cake and set to one side to allow the frosting to dry for about 30 minutes before serving.

A classic American holiday recipe that can be whipped up in no time using shop-bought sweet pastry and tinned pumpkin purée.

pumpkin pie

375 g ready-made sweet pastry

1–2 tablespoons milk

425-g tin puréed pumpkin pie filling (eg Libby's)

2 eggs

1 egg yolk

150 g light brown soft sugar

1 teaspoon ground cinnamon

½ teaspoon ground ginger

a pinch of grated nutmeg

a pinch of ground cloves

a pinch of salt

125 ml double cream

2–3 teaspoons caster sugar

icing sugar, for dusting

a 23-cm round pie dish

a small star-shaped cutter

serves 6

1 Preheat the oven to 180°C (350°F) Gas 4 and place a baking tray on the middle shelf to preheat.

2 Sprinkle a little flour on a clean work surface. Roll out the dough to a thickness of about 2–3 mm. Carefully lift up the pastry (it may help to lift it while on the rolling pin) and lay it in the pie dish. Carefully trim any excess pastry from around the edge with a small knife.

3 Gather up any scraps of dough, knead very lightly to bring together into a ball and roll out again. Use the star-shaped cutter to stamp out lots of stars. Brush the edges of the pie with a little milk and stick the pastry stars, slightly overlapping, all around the edge.

4 Chill the pastry case in the fridge while you prepare the filling.

5 Put the puréed pumpkin, whole eggs and yolk, brown sugar, cinnamon, ginger, nutmeg, cloves, salt and double cream in a large bowl and whisk until well mixed and smooth.

6 Carefully pour the mixture into the pie dish, brush the stars with a little more milk and scatter the caster sugar over them.

7 Ask an adult to help you put the pie on the hot baking tray in the preheated oven. Bake for about 35 minutes, or until the filling has set and the pastry is golden brown.

8 Ask an adult to help you remove the pie from the oven. Leave to cool to room temperature before dusting with icing sugar.

This is a simple fruit cake that can be decorated any number of ways, but with its crown of sparkling, jewelled dried fruits, it makes a beautiful teatime treat.

easy fruit cake

75 g glacé cherries, chopped, plus extra, whole, to decorate

50 g candied mixed peel

450 g mixed dried fruit (eg currants, raisins, sultanas, chopped dried apricots)

225 g plain flour

1 teaspoon baking powder

1 teaspoon mixed spice

a pinch of salt

175 g unsalted butter, softened

175 g caster sugar

3 eggs, lightly beaten

25 g ground almonds

2–3 tablespoons milk

apricot jam, chopped dried apricots, blanched almonds, pecan halves, to decorate

a deep, 20-cm round cake tin

serves 8–10

1 Preheat the oven to 170°C (325°F) Gas 3. **Ask an adult to help you** line the base and side of the cake tin with a double thickness of baking parchment.

2 Mix the chopped glacé cherries, mixed peel and dried fruit together in a bowl.

3 Sift the flour, baking powder, mixed spice and salt together in another bowl.

4 Put the butter and sugar in the bowl of an electric mixer (or use a large bowl and an electric whisk). **Ask an adult to help you** cream them until pale and light.

5 Gradually add the beaten eggs, mixing well between each addition and scraping down the sides of the bowl with a rubber spatula from time to time.

6 Add the dried fruit and stir to mix.

7 Add the sifted dry ingredients and the ground almonds to the mixture and fold in using a large metal spoon or rubber spatula.

8 Add the milk and mix until smooth.

9 Spoon the mixture into the prepared cake tin and spread evenly.

10 Ask an adult to help you put the tin on the middle shelf of the preheated oven. Bake for 30 minutes, then turn the heat down to 150°C (300°F) Gas 2. Continue to bake for a further 1½ hours, or until a skewer inserted into the middle of the cake comes out clean.

11 Ask an adult to help you remove the cake from the oven and leave to cool in the tin.

12 Once the cake is completely cold, tip it out of the tin and carefully peel off the paper.

13 Ask an adult to help you put about 5 tablespoons apricot jam in a small saucepan over low heat. Leave until runny, then sieve.

14 Brush the top of the cake with a thin layer of the jam. Arrange the glacé cherries, apricots and nuts in a pretty pattern on top. Brush with a little more jam to glaze, then leave to set.

This is the perfect cake for a Christmas party,
as it will feed a good crowd of hungry mouths.

Frosty the snowman

Medium Cake (page 8)
Large Cake (page 8)
Buttercream Frosting
  (page 9)
red food colouring paste
300 g desiccated coconut
1 large cupcake (shop-
  bought or home-made)
1 plain liquorice allsort
dark chocolate chips
4 red sugar-coated sweets
40 g white ready-to-use
  fondant or royal icing
orange food colouring
  paste
2 short lengths of flaked
  chocolate

an 18-cm round cake tin,
  greased and base-lined
  with greased baking
  parchment

a 23-cm round cake tin,
  greased and base-lined
  with greased baking
  parchment

a length of ribbon

serves at least 14

1 Preheat the oven to 180°C (350°F) Gas 4.

2 Make up the Medium Cake and Large Cake as described on page 8. Spoon the medium cake batter into the prepared 18-cm cake tin and the large cake batter into the 23-cm cake tin. Spread evenly.

3 Ask an adult to help you put the tins on the middle shelf of the preheated oven. Bake the medium cake for about 30 minutes and the large cake for 35–40 minutes, or until a skewer inserted into the middle of the cakes comes out clean.

4 Ask an adult to help you remove the tins from the oven and leave to cool for 10 minutes before tipping the cakes out to cool on a wire rack.

5 While the cakes are cooling, take the Buttercream Frosting and put 5 tablespoons into a small bowl. Tint this small amount red using the food colouring paste.

6 Lay the cold cakes side by side. If necessary, cut a thin layer off the tops of the cakes so that they are the same height. Cut away about one-fifth off the larger cake in an inward curve and set aside. Lay the ribbon down horizontally before fitting the smaller cake on the ribbon into the curved space.

7 Cover the top and side of both of the cakes in the untinted buttercream, spreading it evenly with a palette knife. Cover the whole cake evenly in desiccated coconut.

8 Use the reserved leaf-shaped piece of cake and the cupcake to make the snowman's hat. Cover these in the red buttercream and position on top of the snowman's head.

9 Cut the liquorice allsort in half for the eyes and arrange the chocolate chips for the mouth. Position the sugar-coated sweets down the centre as buttons.

10 Tint the fondant icing orange using the food colouring paste and shape this into a carrot. Position on the snowman's face.

11 Finally, push a length of flaked chocolate into each side for the snowman's arms.

marble cake

50 g dark chocolate,
   chopped
175 g plain flour
1 rounded teaspoon
   baking powder
175 g unsalted butter,
   softened
200 g caster sugar
4 eggs, lightly beaten
1 teaspoon vanilla extract
2 tablespoons milk
Chocolate Frosting
   (page 9)
chocolate sprinkles

2 x 1-lb. loaf tins, greased

serves 8–10

1 Preheat the oven to 180°C (350°F) Gas 4. Line the base and ends of each loaf tin with a strip of greased baking parchment.

2 Ask an adult to help you put the chocolate in a heatproof bowl over a pan of barely simmering water or in the microwave on a low setting. Stir very carefully until melted.

3 Sift the flour and baking powder together into a bowl.

4 Put the butter and sugar in the bowl of an electric mixer (or use a large bowl and an electric whisk). **Ask an adult to help you** cream them until pale and light.

5 Gradually add the beaten eggs, mixing well between each addition and scraping down the side of the bowl with a rubber spatula from time to time. Add the vanilla extract and mix.

6 Tip the sifted flour and baking powder into the batter and mix until smooth. Stir in the milk. Spoon one-third of this mixture into the melted chocolate. Mix until smooth.

7 Using a tablespoon, drop alternate spoonfuls of vanilla and chocolate batter into one of the prepared loaf tins. When it's half full, give the tin a sharp tap on the work surface to level the mixture. To create a marbled effect, drag the blade of a table knife through the mixture to create swirls. Do not over-swirl the mixture or the effect will not be so dramatic. Repeat this step with the second loaf tin.

8 Ask an adult to help you put the tins on the middle shelf of the preheated oven. Bake for about 40 minutes or until a skewer inserted into the middle of the cakes comes out clean.

9 Ask an adult to help you remove the tins from the oven. Leave to cool for 15 minutes before carefully lifting the cakes out of the tins and onto a wire rack to cool completely.

10 Spread the Chocolate Frosting over the tops of each cold cake and decorate with assorted chocolate sprinkles. You will have some frosting left over – why not use it to frost the Chocolate Brownie Squares on page 12?

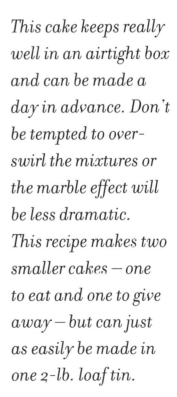

This cake keeps really well in an airtight box and can be made a day in advance. Don't be tempted to over-swirl the mixtures or the marble effect will be less dramatic. This recipe makes two smaller cakes — one to eat and one to give away — but can just as easily be made in one 2-lb. loaf tin.

99

party food

Christmas drinks

hot chocolate

40 g dark chocolate drops
350 ml whole milk
a few drops vanilla extract
2 teaspoons caster sugar
  or honey, or to taste
1 tablespoon whipped
  double cream or squirty
  cream from a can
mini-marshmallows

serves 1

1 Tip the chocolate drops into a heatproof glass or mug.

2 Put the milk, vanilla extract and sugar in a small saucepan. **Ask an adult to help you** set it over medium heat and heat until just boiling, then whisk with a balloon whisk until foamy.

3 Pour the hot milk over the chocolate drops and stir until the chocolate has melted. Taste and add a little more sugar if needed.

4 Dollop the cream on the top, scatter with mini-marshmallows and serve immediately.

mulled apple juice

1 litre cloudy apple juice
1 cinnamon stick
4 whole cloves
2 tablespoons clear honey
1 orange
2–3 small Cox's apples

makes about 4 cups

1 Pour the apple juice into a saucepan and add the cinnamon stick, whole cloves and honey.

2 Remove the zest from the orange in strips using a vegetable peeler and add to the pan.

3 Cut the apples into quarters and remove the cores. Thinly slice the apples and tip them into the apple juice. **Ask an adult to help you** put the pan over medium heat and bring the juice to a gentle simmer. Cook for 5 minutes.

4 Ladle the mulled apple juice into cups or mugs and serve.

These are perfect drinks to warm you up when it's chilly outside. The hot chocolate is made with real chocolate and a few drops of vanilla extract to make it that little bit more special. The mulled apple juice is your opportunity to join in with the adults when they indulge in their own spiced mulled wine!

No party is complete without a heaped dish of hot bite-sized sausage rolls. All you need to add is a bowl of ketchup to serve with them.

sausage rolls

375 g ready-rolled
   puff pastry
1 tablespoon Dijon
   mustard
24 cocktail sausages
1 egg, lightly beaten

*a baking tray, lined with
   baking parchment*

makes 24

1 Preheat the oven to 190°C (375°F) Gas 5.

2 Sprinkle a little flour on a clean work surface. Unroll the pastry, and if it's thicker than 2 mm, use a rolling pin to make it the right thickness. Spread the mustard over the pastry.

3 With the long side of the pastry nearest you, cut the pastry vertically into 6 equal strips. Cut each strip into 4. Place a sausage on each piece of pastry and roll the pastry around it. Arrange on the prepared baking tray.

4 Score 2 or 3 small cuts in the top of each sausage roll with a sharp knife and brush with the beaten egg.

5 Ask an adult to help you put the tray on the middle shelf of the preheated oven. Bake for 30 minutes, or until golden.

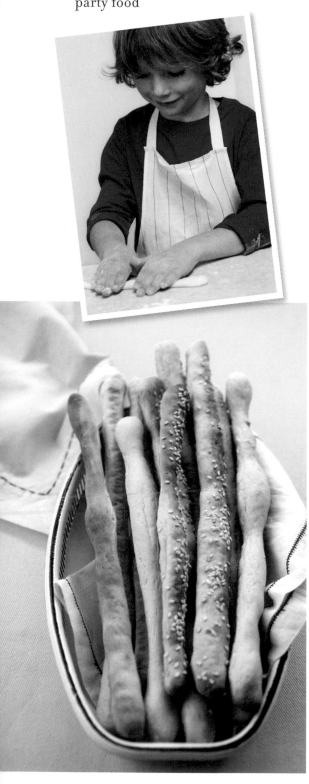

These Italian-style grissini sticks have Parmesan added to the dough to make them a little more interesting. Grissini are delicious eaten on their own or served with dips or soup.

cheesy grissini

375 g strong white flour

1 x 7-g sachet easy-blend dried yeast

1 teaspoon fine sea salt

200 ml warm water

1 tablespoon olive oil

3 tablespoons finely grated Parmesan

1–2 tablespoons sesame seeds (optional)

2 or more baking trays, lined with baking parchment

makes about 24

1 Sift the flour into a large mixing bowl and stir in the yeast and salt. Make a hole like a well in the middle and pour in three-quarters of the water and all the oil. Stir with a wooden spoon – the dough should be soft but not too sticky.

2 Add the grated Parmesan to the dough. It will get mixed in when you knead the dough.

3 To knead the dough, sprinkle a little flour on a clean work surface. Shape the dough into a ball and push on it and press it onto the work surface, turning it round often. You'll need to keep doing this until it is silky smooth and elastic – about 7 minutes.

4 Shape the dough into a neat ball again. Wash and dry the mixing bowl and sit the dough back in it. Cover tightly with clingfilm and leave in a warm place until the dough has doubled in size. This can take at least 1 hour.

5 Preheat the oven to 200°C (400°F) Gas 6.

6 Tip the dough onto the floured work surface and knead for 1 minute. Divide it into walnut-sized pieces and roll each piece into a long stick using your hands. Arrange on the prepared baking trays and leave to rise again for a further 10 minutes.

7 Brush some of the grissini with water and sprinkle the sesame seeds over them, if using.

8 Ask an adult to help you put one of the trays on the middle shelf of the preheated oven. Bake for 7–8 minutes, or until crisp and golden brown.

9 Repeat with the remaining grissini.

This recipe makes a large pot of soup — enough to feed a hungry crowd on a cold winter's day. If you don't like things too spicy, just leave the chilli out.

butternut squash soup with cheesy croutons

1 onion, peeled

1 medium leek

1 celery stick

2 carrots, peeled

25 g unsalted butter

1 tablespoon olive oil

1 butternut squash

1 garlic clove, crushed

1 red chilli, deseeded
   and finely chopped

2 cm fresh ginger, peeled
   and grated

1 litre vegetable stock

sea salt and freshly ground
   black pepper

Croutons

6 slices of 1-day-old bread
   (preferably sourdough)

1 tablespoon olive oil

100 g Cheddar or
   Parmesan, grated

makes a large pot!

1 Ask an adult to help you chop the onion, leek, celery and carrots into small pieces.

2 Put the butter and oil in a large saucepan. Ask an adult to help you set it over medium heat. Add the chopped onion, leek, celery and carrots and cook slowly until they are soft but not browned.

3 While the vegetables are cooking, prepare the butternut squash. Peel the squash – this is quite tricky, so you may need an adult to help you. Cut it in half and scoop out the seeds with a spoon. Cut the flesh into chunks.

4 Add the squash, garlic, chilli and ginger to the pan and continue to cook for a further 3–4 minutes.

5 Add the stock and season with sea salt and freshly ground black pepper. Bring to the boil, then lower the heat so that the soup is at a gentle simmer and continue to cook until the squash is tender.

6 Ask an adult to help you blend the soup until smooth either in a blender or using a stick blender. Check the seasoning and add more salt or pepper if needed. If the soup is a little thick, add some extra stock.

7 To make the croutons, preheat the oven to 180°C (350°F) Gas 4.

8 Cut the bread into chunks and tip into a large bowl. Add the oil and mix with your hands so that the chunks are coated in oil. Add the grated cheese and stir well. Tip the croutons out onto a baking tray.

9 Ask an adult to help you put the tray in the preheated oven. Bake for 15 minutes, or until golden and crisp.

10 Ladle the soup into bowls and scatter some croutons on top. Any leftover soup can be left to cool and then frozen in an airtight box.

French toast is such a nice thing to have as a treat for breakfast. Why not surprise your family and make a batch for everyone early on Christmas morning? You will need just a little help from an adult.

French toast

4 eggs

4 tablespoons milk

a good pinch of ground cinnamon

1 teaspoon vanilla extract

1 tablespoon maple syrup, plus extra for drizzling

12 slices of brioche, white bread or panettone

4 tablespoons unsalted butter

icing sugar, for dusting

a star-shaped cookie cutter

serves 4

1 Put the eggs, milk, cinnamon, vanilla and maple syrup in a mixing bowl and whisk with a balloon whisk.

2 Lay the bread slices out on a chopping board and, using the star-shaped cutter, stamp out a star from the middle of each slice.

3 Ask an adult to help you melt half the butter in a large non-stick frying pan over medium-high heat.

4 Dip half the bread stars into the egg mixture and allow to soak thoroughly on both sides.

5 Add the eggy stars to the hot pan – you will need to fry them in batches because you should have just one layer of stars in the pan at a time. Cook for about 1 minute or until they turn golden.

6 Turn the stars over and cook the other sides for another minute.

7 Repeat with the remaining butter and stars. You will have 3 per person. Dust with icing sugar and drizzle with maple syrup to serve.

buttermilk pancakes

225 g plain flour

3 teaspoons baking
  powder

½ teaspoon salt

4 tablespoons caster sugar

50 g unsalted butter,
  plus extra for frying

125 ml milk

125 ml buttermilk

2 eggs, lightly beaten

1 teaspoon vanilla extract

maple syrup, to serve

crispy rashers of smoked
  bacon, to serve
  (optional)

makes 16–18

1 Sift the flour, baking powder, salt and sugar into a large mixing bowl and make a hole like a well in the middle.

2 Ask an adult to help you melt the butter in a small saucepan over low heat or in the microwave on a low setting.

3 Put the milk, buttermilk, eggs, melted butter and vanilla extract in a jug and whisk with a balloon whisk. Pour into the dry ingredients and whisk until the batter is smooth.

4 Put a knob of butter in a large, heavy frying pan. **Ask an adult to help you** set it over medium heat. Allow the butter to melt,

swirling it so that it coats the bottom of the pan evenly.

5 Drop 4 tablespoons of the pancake batter into the hot pan and cook for about 1 minute, or until bubbles start to appear on the surface. Using a fish slice or palette knife, flip the pancake over and cook the other side until the pancake is golden and well risen. Remove the pancake from the pan and keep it warm on a plate covered with foil.

6 Repeat with the remaining batter.

7 Serve the pancakes with crispy bacon, if you like, and a drizzle of maple syrup.

*What better way to start Christmas morning
than with a mile-high stack of these pancakes?
Serve with a good glug of maple syrup and
rashers of crispy smoked bacon.*

cheese & ham scones

225 g plain flour

**2 teaspoons baking
  powder**

a pinch of salt

**½ teaspoon mustard
  powder (optional)**

**50 g unsalted butter,
  chilled and diced**

**50 g Cheddar, grated, plus
  extra for sprinkling**

50 g ham, diced

1 egg, lightly beaten

75–100 ml milk

a 6-cm round cookie cutter

*a baking tray, lined with
  baking parchment*

makes 8–10

1 Preheat the oven to 200°C (400°F) Gas 6.

2 Sift the flour, baking powder, salt and mustard powder, if using, into a large mixing bowl. Add the chilled, diced butter and rub in using your fingertips.

3 Add three-quarters of the cheese and all the ham and mix well. Make a hole like a well in the middle. Pour in the beaten egg and enough milk to make a soft dough.

4 Sprinkle a little flour on a clean work surface. Use a rolling pin to roll out the dough until it is about 2 cm thick. Stamp out rounds with the cookie cutter and arrange the scones on the prepared baking tray.

5 Brush the scones with a little milk and scatter a little more cheese over the tops. **Ask an adult to help you** put the tray on the middle shelf of the preheated oven. Bake for about 10–12 minutes until golden brown.

6 Ask an adult to help you remove the tray from the oven and tip the scones onto a wire rack to cool.

Scones are so delicious
and so easy to make.
Serve these little
cheesy nuggets still
warm from the oven
or with a bowl of
steaming soup.

You could easily serve these as a fancy starter on Christmas day. The pancakes can be made in advance and frozen – simply wrap them in foil and warm in the oven before serving.

Scotch pancakes with smoked salmon

125 g plain flour

1 teaspoon baking powder

a large pinch of salt

1 egg

150–200 ml milk

1–2 tablespoons sunflower
  oil

To serve

200 g smoked salmon

10 teaspoons crème
  fraîche

1 tablespoon finely
  snipped chives

makes about 20

1 Sift the flour, baking powder and salt into a large mixing bowl. Break the egg into the bowl and gradually pour in the milk, mixing all the time with a balloon whisk. You may not need to add all the milk – the batter should be smooth and thick.

2 Ask an adult to help you preheat a griddle pan or heavy frying pan over medium heat. Pour a little of the oil in the pan and swirl it to coat the base of the pan evenly. Leave it to heat up.

3 Drop a tablespoon of batter into the hot pan for each pancake – you will probably only be able to cook 4 pancakes at a time. Cook for about 1 minute, or until bubbles start to appear on the surface and the underside is golden. Using a fish slice or palette knife, flip the pancakes over and cook the other side until the pancakes are golden.

4 Remove the pancakes from the pan and keep them warm on a plate covered with foil.

5 Repeat with the remaining batter.

6 To serve, snip the smoked salmon into pieces. Dollop ½ teaspoon crème fraîche onto each pancake and top with the salmon. Finish with a sprinkle of snipped chives.

bagel chips

4 plain bagels
3–4 tablespoons olive oil
sea salt flakes
2 teaspoons dried oregano
1 teaspoon smoked
  paprika
2 tablespoons grated
  Parmesan

makes about 32

1 Preheat the oven to 180°C (350°F) Gas 4.

2 Cut each bagel in half to make semi-circles. Put one half cut-side down and very carefully slice the bagel vertically, as thinly as possible. Repeat with the remaining bagels and lay the slices on baking trays in a single layer. Brush each slice with olive oil. Sprinkle a quarter of the slices with salt, a quarter with oregano, a quarter with paprika and a quarter with cheese.

3 Ask an adult to help you bake them in the preheated oven for 15 minutes, or until golden and crisp.

savoury dips

Dips are perfect for parties — serve them with Bagel Chips (page 118) or Cheesy Grissini (page 107).

red pepper & chickpea dip

2 red peppers
2 tablespoons olive
   oil
420-g tin of chickpeas
juice of ½ lemon
1 rounded tablespoon
   Greek yoghurt or
   tahini

1 small garlic clove,
   crushed (optional)
a pinch of cayenne
   pepper (optional)
sea salt and freshly
   ground black
   pepper

makes a bowlful

1 Preheat the grill.

2 Cut the peppers in half and scoop out the seeds with a spoon. Arrange the peppers on a baking tray, skin-side up. Drizzle with the olive oil and **ask an adult to help you** put them under the hot grill. Grill until the skins of the peppers are blackened and charred. Tip the hot peppers into a bowl, cover with clingfilm and leave to cool for about 10 minutes.

3 When the peppers are cool, peel off the skins and throw them away. Put the peppers in the bowl of a food processor. Drain the chickpeas in a sieve and rinse under cold water. Add to the peppers. Add the lemon juice, yoghurt, garlic and cayenne, if using, and season with salt and pepper.

4 **Ask an adult to help you** whizz the ingredients until they are almost smooth. Taste and add more lemon, salt or pepper if you like.

avocado dip

2 ripe avocados
1 ripe tomato
juice of 1 lemon
a dash of
   Worcestershire
   sauce

sea salt and freshly
   ground black
   pepper

makes a bowlful

1 **Ask an adult to help you** cut the avocados in half and remove the stones. Use a spoon to scoop out the flesh from each half and place in a mixing bowl. Mash the avocado with a fork until it is almost smooth.

2 Chop the tomato into small pieces and add to the avocado with the lemon juice and Worcestershire sauce. Mix well, then season with salt and pepper.

cream cheese & herb dip

300 g cream cheese
3 tablespoons Greek
   yoghurt
juice of ½ lemon
1 tablespoon finely
   chopped parsley
1 tablespoons finely
   snipped chives

1 small garlic clove,
   crushed (optional)
sea salt and freshly
   ground black
   pepper

makes a bowlful

1 Put the cream cheese in a mixing bowl and beat with a wooden spoon until slightly softened. Stir in the yoghurt, lemon juice, herbs and garlic, if using. Season to taste with salt and pepper.

Palmiers can be savoury or sweet. These ones are filled with pesto and grated Parmesan, but you could also try scattering the rolled-out pastry with caster sugar and cinnamon.

pesto palmiers

**375 g ready-rolled
    puff pastry**
2 tablespoons red pesto
2 tablespoons green pesto
100 g Parmesan, grated
50 g Cheddar, finely grated
1 egg, beaten

makes about 24

1 Sprinkle a little flour on a clean work surface. Use a rolling pin to roll out the dough to a rectangle just over 50 x 25 cm. Using a large knife, trim the edges of the rectangle and then cut the pastry in half lengthways to give 2 squares measuring roughly 25 x 25 cm.

2 Spread the red pesto over one square and green pesto over the other. Scatter some grated Parmesan and Cheddar evenly over each square of pastry.

3 Take one square and fold the sides in towards the middle until they meet. Brush the top with a little beaten egg. Fold the sides in again to meet in the middle, then brush with more egg and fold in again. The pastry should now be in a long, thin roll. Place on a baking tray and set aside while you do the same with the other square of pastry.

4 Chill the rolls in the fridge for 30 minutes.

5 Preheat the oven to 180°C (350°F) Gas 4.

6 Cut the pastry rolls into 1-cm slices and arrange the slices in a single layer on 2 baking trays. Slightly flatten each palmier. **Ask an adult to help you** put one tray on the middle shelf of the oven. Bake for about 20 minutes, or until golden and crisp.

7 Repeat to bake the second tray of palmiers.

Cheesy and just a little bit spicy, these straws are nice with a mug of Mulled Apple Juice (page 102).

These nuts can be made well in advance and stored in an airtight container. Use unsalted and unroasted nuts from the baking section of the supermarket and feel free to vary the selection to include hazelnuts and walnuts, if you prefer.

spiced mixed nuts

200 g shelled Brazil nuts
100 g shelled almonds
100 g shelled pecan nuts
½ teaspoon cayenne
pepper
½ teaspoon ground
cinnamon
2 tablespoons olive oil
2 teaspoons golden caster
sugar
½ teaspoon sea salt flakes
freshly ground black pepper

serves 6

1 Preheat the oven to 190°C (375°F) Gas 5.

2 Mix all the ingredients together well.

3 Spread evenly in a single layer on a baking tray. **Ask an adult to help you** put the tray on the middle shelf of the oven. Bake for about 10 minutes, or until golden and crisp.

4 Ask an adult to help you remove the tray from the oven and leave to cool slightly before serving.

cheese straws

125 g plain flour
a pinch of sea salt
½ teaspoon cayenne
pepper
½ teaspoon mustard
powder
100 g unsalted butter,
chilled and diced
100 g mixed grated mature
Cheddar and Parmesan

a baking tray, lined with
baking parchment

makes about 24

1 Sift the flour, salt, cayenne and mustard powder into the bowl of a food processor. Add the butter. **Ask an adult to help you** pulse the ingredients until they look like breadcrumbs.

2 Add the grated cheeses and pulse again until the dough starts to come together into a ball.

3 To knead the dough, sprinkle a little flour on a clean work surface. Shape the dough into a ball and push on it and press it onto the work surface. Do this very briefly, just to bring the dough together. Flatten into a disc, cover with clingfilm and chill in the fridge for 30 minutes.

4 Preheat the oven to 190°C (375°F) Gas 5.

5 Tip the dough onto the floured work surface and roll out with a rolling pin until it is about 6–7 mm thick. Cut into 1-cm wide strips and arrange on the prepared baking tray.

6 Ask an adult to help you put the tray on the middle shelf of the oven. Bake for about 12 minutes, or until golden.

7 Ask an adult to help you remove the tray from the oven and leave to cool slightly before serving.

123

These knotted little bread rolls are so easy and delicious. They can be left plain or scattered with sesame seeds, poppy seeds or grated cheese before baking. They're yummy with a bowl of Butternut Squash Soup (page 108).

pretzels

300 g strong white flour

1 teaspoon caster sugar

1 teaspoon easy-blend
   dried yeast

½ teaspoon salt, plus extra
   for sprinkling

150 ml milk

1 tablespoon sunflower oil

1 egg yolk, lightly beaten

1 tablespoon poppy seeds

1 tablespoon sesame seeds

2 baking trays, lined with
   baking parchment

makes 8

1 Tip the flour, sugar, yeast and salt into a large mixing bowl and make a hole like a well in the middle.

2 Put the milk in a small saucepan. **Ask an adult to help you** put the pan over low heat and heat up until the milk is warm. Stir the oil into the warm milk.

3 Pour the warm milk mixture into the well in the dry ingredients and mix with a wooden spoon until the ingredients come together into a dough.

4 To knead the dough, first sprinkle a little flour on a clean work surface. Then shape the dough into a ball and push on it and press it onto the work surface, turning it round often. You'll need to keep doing this until it is silky smooth and elastic – this will take about 8 minutes and you may need to add more flour if the dough is too sticky.

5 Shape the dough into a neat ball again. Wash and dry the mixing bowl and sit the dough back in it. Cover tightly with clingfilm

and leave in a warm place until the dough has doubled in size. This can take at least 1 hour.

6 Tip the dough onto the floured work surface and knead for 1 minute. Divide into 8 equal pieces. Roll each piece into a 40-cm long rope. Twist the dough rope into a knot and place on one of the prepared baking trays.

7 Lightly oil a large sheet of clingfilm, then use it to loosely cover the baking trays (oiled-side down). Leave in a warm place to rise again for a further 30 minutes.

8 Preheat the oven to 190°C (375°F) Gas 5.

9 Gently brush the pretzels with the egg yolk and sprinkle with salt, poppy or sesame seeds.

10 **Ask an adult to help you** put the baking trays on the middle shelf of the preheated oven. Bake for about 15 minutes or until deep golden.

11 **Ask an adult to help you** remove the trays from the oven and leave to cool for a few minutes before tipping out onto a wire rack.

index

acknowledgements

I would like to say an enormous thank you to a few special people who have made this book so beautiful. To Lisa Linder for her fabulous pictures and to Liz Belton for her creative props and tableware – you are both a joy to work with! And to Céline and Megan at Ryland Peters & Small for putting the whole package together so wonderfully – as always.

And a big festive thank you to everyone who modelled, stirred, baked and tasted on the photoshoots, and gave their seal of approval to the recipes.

And to Mungo, who sits patiently in his basket (on a good day) and waits until it's time for dinner and a long walk across the fields.

The publisher would like to thank the lovely models who appear in this book: Charlie; Constance and Lydia; Mackie; Thomas and Ollie; Celia, Max & Timmy; Polly and Will; Ella and Ben; Bella; Emma and Julian; Marly; Bluebelle; Imani and India; Malise; David; Saffron and Parisa.

128

Contents

▶ **List of Auschwitz internees.**
The Nazis kept detailed records of the prisoners selected for work-duty.

Oswiecim

Oswiecim is a small town in the south of Poland, about 50 kilometres west of Krakow, on the main Krakow-Vienna railway line.

Poland has a turbulent history. Although it has existed for centuries, its neighbours have fought over it repeatedly, claiming that it really belonged to them. However, after the First World War (1914-18), these disputes appeared to be over: Poland was guaranteed independent status as a country in its own right.

Oswiccim had been little affected by outside events. Life there in the first half of the twentieth century carried on in much the same way as it had for some 100 years. It was a quiet market town.

But, in 1939, Nazi Germany invaded Poland – and so began the Second World War. While most people's attention was focused on the war, in sleepy Oswiecim the Nazis were quietly and ruthlessly carrying out the systematic murder of over a million people. When the world discovered what they had done, this small town became better known by its German name – Auschwitz.

Today Auschwitz and the death camp the Nazis built there stand as a horrifying symbol of the worst that human beings can do. So what really happened? How did the Nazis manage mass-murder on such a scalc? How did they justify it? These questions and more are explored in this book.

◀ **Oswiecim today.** Stand today in the fields outside Oswiecim and look in one direction: you can see the small town in the distance. Turn in the opposite direction, and you can see the remains of the death camp that the Nazis built there. ▼

▲ **Old Oswiecim.** Before the Second World War, Oswiecim was an attractive little town with its fair share of fine buildings and cobbled streets.

The Nazis Invade Poland

The Nazis had planned their invasion of Poland for a long time. When they came to power in 1933, their leader Adolf Hitler made it very clear that he thought Germany had a right to take over countries in Eastern Europe to provide more land – room to live or "Lebensraum" – for the German people.

Hitler justified his claims on the grounds of supposed German racial superiority. He never made any secret of his contempt for the Slavs: the Poles and other peoples of Eastern Europe. His racist theory argued that the German "Aryan" race deserved to be in control and that "lower" racial groups – including the Slavs – should be ordered what to do.

Although the Western Allies declared war on Germany to uphold Poland's independence, they could not stop the Nazis' efficient takeover. The invasion was so swift and Poland so poor that the Poles didn't stand a chance. They fought bravely against the terrifying power of Hitler's "Blitzkrieg" – lightning war. Blitzkrieg used aircraft to bomb enemy towns and soften up resistance before a massive advance of tanks and infantry. Poland was still using cavalry charges. Their army was quickly defeated.

The Nazis could now put their ideas into action and settle Germans in Poland. They also faced another decision: what to do about the 3.3 million Jews in Poland?

▲ **German tanks.** Since coming to power in 1933, Hitler had been experimenting with new and highly efficient systems of warfare, training up a powerful fighting machine. By 1939 he was ready for war.

▲ Polish cavalry.
Many people across Europe hoped that the horrors of the First World War would ensure an end to all war. As a result, few were prepared for another outbreak of hostilities. What's more, countries like Poland were largely reliant on out-of-date practices and weaponry. Faced with attack by tanks, Poland still relied on cavalry charges.

▶ Poland surrenders.
Within weeks of the invasion and despite courageous fighting by the Poles, the German army was utterly victorious and official Polish resistance was swiftly crushed.

A Problem the Nazis Created

The Nazis' racial theories taught that Jews especially were to be despised. They blamed them for all that was wrong in Europe. As soon as the Nazis took power in Germany, they instituted a series of anti-Jewish laws. Jews were restricted in the jobs they could do and where they could go.

The Nazis also persuaded the German population that "foreign" Jews didn't belong. Jews whose parents were born abroad were simply "dumped" on the border. Many fled east, to Poland, which already had a large Jewish population. When Germany invaded Poland, it found itself in control of over 3 million Jews. All, according to the Nazis, were enemies of the state.

In occupied Poland, the Nazis forced Jews to live in particular areas of the main cities – the ghettoes. These were enclosed like a prison and people could only leave with a permit. The living conditions inside the ghettoes were terrible – too many people crowded together without enough food. Many died.

But this was not enough for the Nazis. They wanted to wipe out the Jews altogether. Their first attempts were savage but inefficient: SS killing squads roamed the countryside rounding up and shooting Jews; but according to Hitler's deputy Himmler, this was "not suitable for liquidating large numbers of people in a short space of time". At the Wannsee conference in January 1942, the Nazi leaders agreed plans for "a Final Solution to the Jewish Problem" and a policy of extermination across the whole of occupied Europe. To achieve this, they realised they would have to find the most efficient system of killing ever invented.

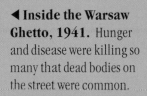

◄ **"Jews are not wanted in this place!"** Signs like this one in Schwedt in Germany were erected wherever the Nazis took power. In general, the local population went along with such visible anti-semitism.

▲ **An early round-up.** The Nazi authorities regularly went into the ghettoes and rounded up selected people for transport East. Usually those selected were told that they were going to labour camps.

▼ **The yellow star**, which Jews were forced to wear.

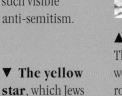
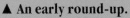

◄ **Inside the Warsaw Ghetto, 1941.** Hunger and disease were killing so many that dead bodies on the street were common.

► **The Jews of Europe.** In January 1942, Hitler's advisers met at Wannsee, near Berlin, and discussed how many Jews they would have to kill in their "Final Solution". This actual list was presented, showing the number of Jews in each country, even including countries the Nazis had not yet conquered.

L a n d		Zahl
A. Altreich		131.800
Ostmark		43.700
Ostgebiete		420.000
Generalgouvernement		2.284.000
Bialystok		400.000
Protektorat Böhmen und Mähren		74.200
Estland — judenfrei —		
Lettland		3.500
Litauen		34.000
Belgien		43.000
Dänemark		5.600
Frankreich / Besetztes Gebiet		165.000
Unbesetztes Gebiet		700.000
Griechenland		69.600
Niederlande		160.800
Norwegen		1.300
B. Bulgarien		48.000
England		330.000
Finnland		2.300
Irland		4.000
Italien einschl. Sardinien		58.000
Albanien		200
Kroatien		40.000
Portugal		3.000
Rumänien einschl. Bessarabien		342.000
Schweden		8.000
Schweiz		18.000
Serbien		10.000
Slowakei		88.000
Spanien		6.000
Türkei (europ. Teil)		55.500
Ungarn		742.800
UdSSR		5.000.000
Ukraine	2.994.684	
Weißrußland ausschl. Bialystok	446.484	
Zusammen: über		11.000.000

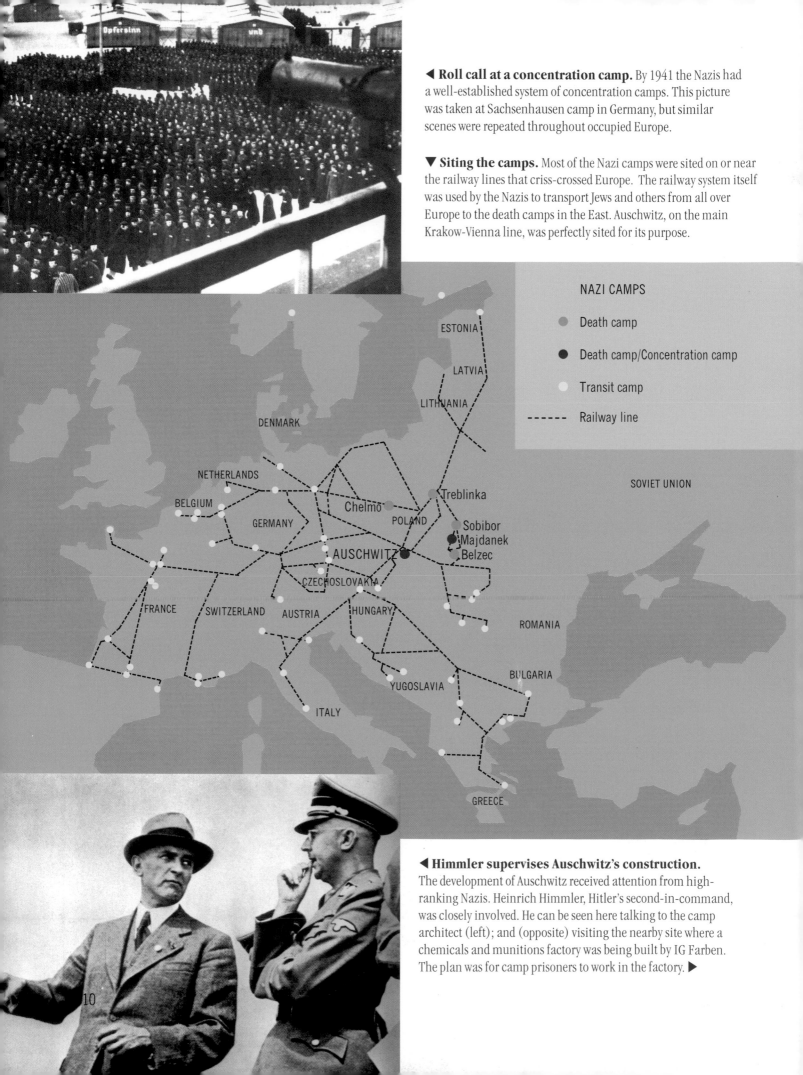

◄ **Roll call at a concentration camp.** By 1941 the Nazis had a well-established system of concentration camps. This picture was taken at Sachsenhausen camp in Germany, but similar scenes were repeated throughout occupied Europe.

▼ **Siting the camps.** Most of the Nazi camps were sited on or near the railway lines that criss-crossed Europe. The railway system itself was used by the Nazis to transport Jews and others from all over Europe to the death camps in the East. Auschwitz, on the main Krakow-Vienna line, was perfectly sited for its purpose.

NAZI CAMPS

- Death camp
- Death camp/Concentration camp
- Transit camp
- ----- Railway line

ESTONIA
LATVIA
LITHUANIA
DENMARK
NETHERLANDS
BELGIUM
GERMANY
Chelmo
POLAND
Treblinka
Sobibor
Majdanek
Belzec
AUSCHWITZ
SOVIET UNION
CZECHOSLOVAKIA
FRANCE
SWITZERLAND
AUSTRIA
HUNGARY
ROMANIA
YUGOSLAVIA
BULGARIA
ITALY
GREECE

◄ **Himmler supervises Auschwitz's construction.**
The development of Auschwitz received attention from high-ranking Nazis. Heinrich Himmler, Hitler's second-in-command, was closely involved. He can be seen here talking to the camp architect (left); and (opposite) visiting the nearby site where a chemicals and munitions factory was being built by IG Farben. The plan was for camp prisoners to work in the factory. ▶

10

An Ideal Site

The Wannsee conference may have finalised the Nazis' plans, but the preparations for a death camp at Auschwitz had already begun.

Soon after taking over Poland, the Nazis had identified an old army barracks at Auschwitz as an almost ready-made concentration camp – a form of prison in which large numbers could be held using very few guards. The Nazis were already using such camps in Germany to deal with their opponents. The over-crowding and poor hygiene meant that many died of malnutrition and disease.

To construct the camp, the Nazis surrounded the Auschwitz barracks with barbed wire and electrified fences, established sentry towers, and moved in a handful of guards to run it under the orders of senior Nazi officers. German convicts were employed as guards. They could be relied on to do whatever was asked in order to continue to benefit from the privilege of being freed. Within a few months the first part of Auschwitz was established as a concentration camp, mainly for Polish political prisoners.

The Nazi leaders took a keen interest in the development of Auschwitz, perhaps because they had already spotted its potential as a substantial and important camp. Auschwitz was more or less in the middle of Europe and easily accessible by rail from all over the continent. It was also some distance from major centres; no-one need see what went on there.

Dusch- und Waschräume

Einer der großen Schlafsäle. An den Betten die angebrachten Eß- und Trinkgeschirre

Sanitätsstube

▲ **A camp to be proud of.**
This page from a brochure about the Oranienburg concentration camp indicates that the Nazis were not ashamed of the camps they built. They believed the harsh regime was something to boast about.

The Plans

Enlargement showing part of Auschwitz II.
These rows and rows of barrack huts each accommodated several hundred prisoners. ▼

Crematoria and gas chambers

Crematoria and gas chambers

"LOOT" STORAGE (B-IIG)

PRISONER'S HOSPITAL (B-IIF)

GYPSY CAMP (B-IIE)

MEN'S CAMP (B-IID)

HUNGARIAN CAMP (B-IIC)

B-III SECTION

FAMILY CAMP (B-IIB)

QUARANTINE CAMP (B-IIA)

THE RAMP

RAILCARS

▲ **Himmler inspects the plans.**
Although Auschwitz grew very quickly, its growth was carefully planned and each development was thoroughly worked out for maximum efficiency.

▶ **The barrack huts.**
The vast majority of prisoners who entered the gates of Auschwitz-Birkenau (Auschwitz II) never saw the inside of these huts: they were killed on arrival.

That first part of the camp, known as Auschwitz I, was fairly small. Within a few months though, in the autumn of 1941, a further section of the camp was built, near the little village of Birkenau. This was sometimes called Auschwitz-Birkenau and sometimes Auschwitz II. Soon after, a third section of the camp was built – Auschwitz III.

The prisoners in Auschwitz I and III were mostly used as slave labour. A huge chemicals/munitions factory owned by IG Farben had been built nearby to make use of this work force. Prisoners also laboured in other local factories and quarries. Some had to help run the camps, too.

Originally Auschwitz II (Auschwitz-Birkenau) contained more barracks, particularly for Soviet prisoners (after the Nazi invasion of the USSR in 1941), and then Jews. However, from the start, some of its inmates were simply being killed.

From 1942 onwards, Jews from all over Europe were being sent there in their thousands to be killed by poisonous gas. This was originally done in an adapted farmhouse but, by 1943, special purpose-built gas chambers were installed. In 1944 the railway was extended closer to the gas chambers to speed up the killing.

▶ **The Auschwitz-Birkenau complex.**
This air reconnaisance photo taken by the Allies in 1944 shows the huge scale of Auschwitz. It had three main camps and in its few years of operation "processed" literally millions of people.

12

Auschwitz-Birkenau
(Auschwitz II)

SS barracks

Auschwitz I

Railway line

River Vistula

IG Farben chemicals/
munitions factory

Auschwitz III

13

> Every block, for instance, had a 'block-elder'. They could boss you around at will, and they were the people who arranged for the collection of bread for the block from the kitchen and distributed it. The loaves were cut into four portions, and what could have been easier than to make those portions a bit undersized and keep the rest for your own purposes? That was where the camp currency came from. The camp had a highly developed hierarchy and was run almost entirely by it. To be a Kapo or a block-elder meant that you belonged to the aristocracy. Anita Lasker-Wallfisch

Camp Organisation

The Auschwitz camps were run as an efficient machine. Nothing was wasted. The SS, the elite force of the Nazi regime, managed the whole process. They controlled the initial arrival of prisoners – and selected who should live and who should go straight to the gas chambers (the majority). They supervised those working in the camp, including ordinary soldiers, convicts from other jails and prisoners; and also the prisoners selected for hard labour.

Many prisoners were employed in the camp itself to dispose of the dead bodies and sort the leftover possessions. Items taken from prisoners were carefully stored for possible reuse: artificial limbs could be sent to the German war-wounded; shoes were valuable; even the prisoners' shaved head-hair was saved to stuff mattresses or make socks.

Prisoner-workers were controlled by other prisoners who took on such roles in exchange for special privileges. Jobs which gave access to medicines or food were particularly sought after. Convicts released from jail were often used to supervise other prisoners on work-duty. They were known as "Kapos" and were among the most ruthless "officers" in the system.

▲ **Adolf Eichmann.** A Nazi official who helped to organise the extermination of the Jews. He came to Auschwitz towards the end of the war to ensure the process was speeded up.

▶**Prisoners' possessions**. Vast quantities of goods were taken from arriving prisoners. They included jewellery, gold teeth and other valuables, but also quite ordinary items. All were kept to be sent to Germany for reuse.

▲ **Prisoner-workers.** Prisoners selected for labour were registered in a meticulous system of record-keeping. At first they were photographed; later, to save time, they were tattooed with a number. Those prisoners who were taken to the gas chambers immediately on arrival were not recorded.

15

Found at Auschwitz.
When the camp was liberated in 1945, piles and piles of prisoners' possessions were found there, including:

thousands of suitcases...

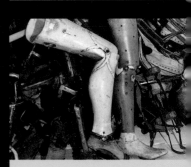

thousands of artificial limbs...

thousands of shoes...

mountains of human hair...

thousands of toothbrushes.

The Transports

By the end of 1941 Auschwitz was set up to receive prisoners, mainly Jews, from all over Nazi-controlled Europe. Exploiting the excellent rail network, the Nazis ensured that Jews in many different countries were rounded up and transported there. Most often they were sent in cattle trucks or sealed freight cars, with as many as 100-150 people crammed into each one.

The first transports to arrive were from Poland and all of these Jews were immediately killed. In March 1942, transports arrived from Slovakia and France. The first transports from Holland came in July, and further transports in 1942 came mainly from Belgium, Yugoslavia, Norway and Germany.

In 1943 transports also arrived from Greece, Italy, Latvia and Austria, while in 1944 most arriving prisoners came from the large Jewish community in Hungary, the last to be liquidated.

Occasionally, Jews were brought from other communities, too, and many non-Jews were also sent to Auschwitz, including at least 60,000 non-Jewish Poles, 119,000 Gypsies and 12,000 Soviet prisoners of war.

On arrival the vast majority of prisoners went straight to the gas chambers. For example, on one day, from an arrival of 1,710 deportees from Holland, 1,594 were immediately gassed, and only 116 were sent to the barracks.

▲ **In France, 1943.** French Jews were rounded up, in some cases even before the Nazi occupiers asked for them, and were sent to death camps in the East.

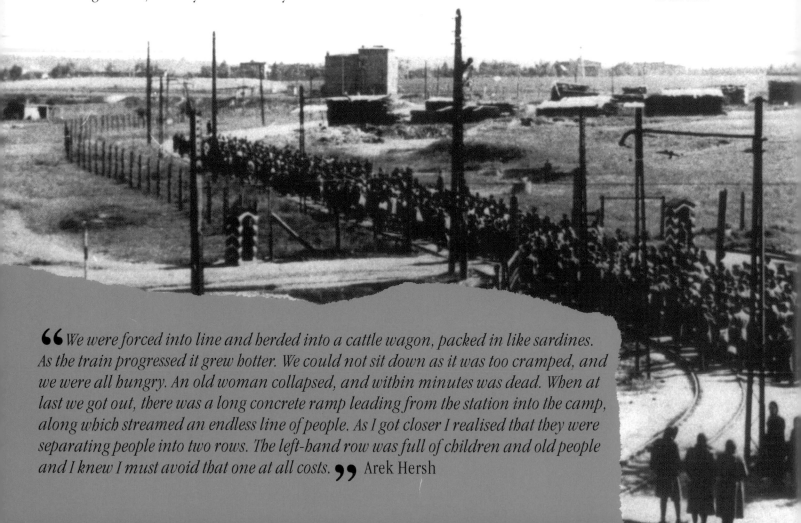

We were forced into line and herded into a cattle wagon, packed in like sardines. As the train progressed it grew hotter. We could not sit down as it was too cramped, and we were all hungry. An old woman collapsed, and within minutes was dead. When at last we got out, there was a long concrete ramp leading from the station into the camp, along which streamed an endless line of people. As I got closer I realised that they were separating people into two rows. The left-hand row was full of children and old people and I knew I must avoid that one at all costs. Arek Hersh

▼ **In Hungary, 1944.** Hungarian Jews were among the last to be rounded up. In a desperate last-minute bid, even as Germany was losing the war, Eichmann and others rushed to Hungary to speed up the transportation of Jews to Auschwitz. Hundreds of thousands were killed in the last few months of the war.

◀ **Walking to the station, Poland, 1943.** In many rural areas Jews were rounded up and marched to the nearest station to board the trains. Sometimes they had to walk for several days, carrying their suitcases with them.

▲ **Boarding the train, Poland, 1943.** Cattle and goods trucks from all over Europe were used to transport prisoners to the death camps. Prisoners were crowded into them without food, water or sanitation, and sent on journeys often lasting several days. Many prisoners died on the way.

The Selection Process

Auschwitz was never designed to accommodate all the prisoners sent there. What's more, there was no desire to keep most of the prisoners alive. In particular Auschwitz II was specifically developed to kill the maximum number of Jews as quickly as possible.

However, the Nazis recognised that it could be profitable to use some of the prisoners as slave labour for at least a period of time.

▼ **Arriving at the camp.** Prisoners emerged from the overcrowded cattle trucks onto a ramp. They were immediately hustled into a line, usually five abreast, for the selection process.

> 66 *When we arrived, they did not interrogate everybody, only a few. And on the basis of the replies, they pointed in two different directions. Someone dared to ask for his luggage: they replied: 'luggage afterwards'. Someone else did not want to leave his wife: they said, 'together again afterwards'. Mothers did not want to leave their children: they said, 'Good, good, stay with child'. They behaved calmly, like people doing normal jobs. In less than 10 minutes all the fit men had been selected. From our convoy, 96 men and 29 women entered Auschwitz I and Auschwitz III. Of the more than 500 others, not one was living two days later.* 99 Primo Levi

Therefore, as soon as the transports arrived, prisoners were made to stand in line and a selection process took place.

Those who were judged capable of hard work were told to go to one side (the right): on average about 20 per cent of the arrivals. The remainder – the old, the infirm, children with their mothers and any apparently weaker people – were sent to the left and immediately taken to the gas chambers and killed.

No attempt was made to record this instantly condemned 80 per cent. We can only estimate the number of people who were immediately killed by referring to the fact that so many are known to have been sent to Auschwitz who were never seen alive again. Usual estimates range from 1.5 million to 4 million people murdered at Auschwitz.

▼ **Selected for labour.** A small proportion of prisoners, mostly men but also some young women, were selected for hard labour either in the quarries or in the factories.

Making the selection. SS officers divided the arriving prisoners into two groups. Most women, children and elderly people were sent to the left – for immediate progress to the "showers" (the gas chambers) and death.

19

The Cleansing Routine

Prisoners arriving at Auschwitz experienced one of two routines. Both were done in a matter-of-fact way that suggested "normality".

Those who had been chosen for the gas chambers were told that they would be going for a shower, to be deloused before rejoining their families. Their luggage was taken from them and piled on the ramp. They were led into a large changing room where they took off their clothes and folded them tidily for when they returned.

They were then herded into one of the gas chambers at Auschwitz II, and killed. Usually, between 2,000 and 2,500 people were gassed at a time.

Those who had been selected for hard labour or other work had their head shaved; they were made to change out of their clothes into prison uniform; their photograph was taken or a number was tattooed on their forearm. They also had to hand over their luggage.

In general, when Jews were rounded up for transportation to Auschwitz, they were encouraged to think that they were going to a work camp or to be resettled in the East, and they were told to bring with them a small bag of possessions. This not only made people more co-operative but it also ensured that valuable items were brought to Auschwitz which the Nazis could then steal.

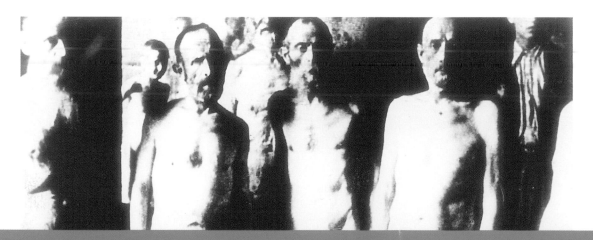

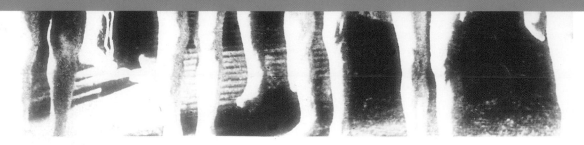

▲ **Outside the gas chambers.** Prisoners were required to strip off before entering the gas chambers. They were told they were going to have a shower. This rare picture, smuggled out by a camp inmate, shows a group of prisoners waiting to enter the gas chambers.

66 *They tattooed me and they told us, from now on, this is your name. My name was A-5143. Your name was your number. I felt like I was not a human person anymore. They had shaved our heads and I felt so ashamed and also when they told us to undress, they made us feel like animals. The men were walking around and laughing and looking at us. I wanted the ground to open up and for me to be swallowed by it.* 99 Lily Malnick

▲ **Women prisoners on parade.** Those women selected to live had their hair shaved off and a number tattooed on their arm. They spent hours standing on parade. Many women, particularly non-Jewish prisoners, worked as slave labourers in the nearby factories.

▶ **Organised plunder.** One of the jobs to be done at Auschwitz was sorting through the possessions of newly arrived prisoners.

21

The Gas Chambers

As early as 1940, the Nazis had already experimented with gassing prisoners by locking them in the back of a van and redirecting the exhaust fumes into the van. Then, in September 1941, Soviet prisoners of war and others who were ill were herded down into a cellar in Auschwitz and killed there with poisonous gas. This poison-gas was the fumes from prussic acid and was known under the trade name of Zyklon B.

Mass murders by gas started in Auschwitz II – Birkenau – at the beginning of 1942 in a specially adapted farmhouse. By early 1943, purpose-built gas chambers disguised as showers had been built, so more Jews could be killed more quickly.

The gas chambers were tiled rooms with shower heads in the ceiling. But instead of water, poison-gas was pumped in through holes in the ceiling. Once all the prisoners were dead, special teams of prisoner-workers known as the "Sonderkommando" dragged the bodies out and took them away for disposal.

At times prisoners arrived too fast for the gas chambers to cope with, which put the whole camp under considerable pressure. This was especially true in the last year of the war when the Nazis accelerated their transports to Auschwitz.

▶ **Waiting for death.** This group of Hungarian Jews wait to go to the gas chambers which can be glimpsed just beyond the trees. They are probably unaware of their fate.

▶ **Gas canisters.** Zyklon B was the specially developed poison-gas used in the gas chambers at Auschwitz. It came in the form of pellets which released poisonous gas when exposed to air.

> **❝** *They took us to a shower. They asked us to put our shoes together, tie our shoelaces together and put our clothes down. But it turned out that the shower was really the gas. I know only that it was dark, that the Germans were terribly nervous, that when it didn't work and we came out they were very angry, shouting, 'This has never happened before!' The block-elder looked at us and started to scream, 'How could it happen? Why are you back? You're not supposed to be back.' I think that was the only time in Auschwitz that the gas did not work.* **❞**
>
> Alice Lok

▼ **Russian soldiers with gas canisters.** When Auschwitz was liberated, large numbers of abandoned gas canisters were found in the camp. These Russian soldiers are posing with some of them as evidence of what had been done at Auschwitz.

Burning the Bodies

The thousands of prisoners who arrived at Auschwitz each day and were gassed there presented the Nazis with a further problem. It was impossible to bury the bodies quickly enough; they had to find some other method to dispose of them.

To cope with this, special crematoria were built at Auschwitz II with huge banks of ovens that enabled hundreds of bodies to be burnt at a time.

On some occasions, however, even keeping the crematoria going at full blast could not keep pace with the mounting death toll. For this reason, some bodies were buried in large mass graves and others were disposed of in quicklime pits. (Quicklime works like a kind of acid: it reacts with the water in the human body, reducing it to dust.)

The bodies of those who had been gassed were not the only ones to be burnt; every day there were also many among the camp labourers who died from overwork, malnutrition and disease, and were disposed of in the crematoria.

Special groups of prisoners, the Sonderkommando, were forced to do the work of feeding the bodies into the ovens. Some of them buried accounts of what they had seen and what they had been made to do. The Sonderkommando also scattered human teeth around the camp to leave some evidence of the huge numbers of people killed.

" All the crematoria were working at full blast. Last night they burned the Greek Jews [from Corfu]. The victims were kept for 27 days without food or water, first in launches, then in sealed boxcars. When they arrived at Auschwitz, the doors were unlocked, but no one got out and lined up for selection. Half of them were already dead, and the other half in a coma. The entire convoy was sent straight to number two crematorium. Later I noticed that the four lightning rods, placed on the crematorium chimneys, were twisted and bent due to the previous night's high temperatures. "

From the journal of Miklos Nyiszli

◀ Crematorium building. One of the four specially-built brick crematoria at Auschwitz. The crematoria were kept going day and night to dispose of the remains of victims. It is estimated that, at Auschwitz, 8,000 bodies could be burnt every 24 hours.

▲ Too many bodies. Sometimes so many people were killed in the gas chambers that the crematoria could not burn them all straightaway. When this happened, bodies were stacked in rows, for burial or burning at a later time.

▲ The ovens. Inside the crematoria were banks of ovens, each large enough to accommodate a human body. The fires were kept stoked up day and night as body after body was loaded in and turned to ashes.

▼ Burning bodies. This blurred photograph was one of seven smuggled out by the camp inmates themselves. It shows the Sonderkommando burning bodies out of doors because the crematoria were full to capacity.

25

A Living Death

A small proportion of those transported to Auschwitz were selected as being temporarily useful – to be worked to death, literally, as slave labour.

These inmates were housed in barracks in various parts of the camp. They slept in overcrowded bunks which looked more like shelves. There was no proper bedding or heating, and the Polish winters were icy cold. Food rations consisted of a small amount of bread and some thin soup each day. Nowhere was there any colour; the whole place seemed totally grey and lifeless.

The overcrowded conditions, the shortage of water rations and the lack of any proper toilet or washing facilities meant that most prisoners were vulnerable to dysentery and typhoid. Becoming too weak to work was a death sentence.

Punishments were frequent and for the slightest reason – for example, being late for roll-call (inspection parade). Prisoners were beaten and whipped and even executed in front of the rest of the inmates. Roll-call was taken frequently, often into the night. Hours and hours of standing in rows in the freezing cold took their toll, and many prisoners did not survive such treatment.

With no news from the outside world, prisoners had no idea whether there was any point in hoping for freedom or not. Suicide was not uncommon.

▲ **Inside a barrack hut at Auschwitz.** Inmates were not only stacked up on three-tiered bunks but usually each bed was shared by several prisoners. They rarely had mattresses or blankets, there was no heating, and the Polish winters were bitterly cold.

▶ **The torture chamber.** This door led to one of the most dreaded places in Auschwitz, where prisoners were taken to betray their fellows.

▼ **Punishment.** This Russian prisoner of war was strapped in a standing position until he could stand upright no longer. Prisoners who survived such punishment were expected to work immediately after.

> *It was Yom Kippur [a Jewish fast day] and so I had eaten nothing. When I asked for a little extra in the evening, they punished me. The upper part of my body was put in an oven of the type they had there in Auschwitz II and I was beaten on the lower part of my body, with a stick which was very thick, which they used to carry the lunch pails. At first they gave me ten strokes. I fainted: water was poured on me: then another ten blows: I fainted again – again they revived me, until I received twenty-five blows.*
>
> Nahum Hoch

▼A suicide. For some prisoners, trying to survive became too much. Sometimes prisoners would throw themselves onto the electrified fence and end it all.

27

Slave Labour

We can only estimate the number of prisoners sent to Auschwitz who went straight to the gas chambers. However, the group selected to live is well documented and there is plenty of information about their lives from the few who actually survived. Most were used for slave labour.

An early development at Auschwitz was the building of the IG Farben factory, which produced materials for the German war effort. It and other local factories used slave labourers. They would be marched daily from Auschwitz to the factory, and there work a 12-hour shift with few if any breaks. Most civilian workers preferred to ignore the skeletal prisoners who turned up each day.

Other prisoners worked in quarries, where injury and death were common.

Though slave labour was preferable to the other options, by 1944 conditions had deteriorated further. As German defeat loomed, the slave labourers were forced to work harder and longer, living in increasingly overcrowded conditions, and always vulnerable to disease. In Auschwitz, any prisoner not fit to work would simply be sent to the gas chamber — and everyone knew it.

> *They would take us outside to move huge rocks. One day we would take these huge rocks from this side and carry them to that side. The next day, they would bring us back; and we would take these same huge rocks, and carry them from that side back to this side. Now you need to know that we were undernourished. We were all weak. By the time they took us back to the barracks at night we could barely crawl. But we needed to show that we could still walk, that we were strong enough to give one more day.* Fritzie Fritshall

▼ **Women slave labourers.** These women are being marched off to their day's work in one of the nearby factories. In general, until near the end of the war, this was one of the better options at Auschwitz: slave factory workers received more rations and were at least indoors for much of the day.

▶**Hard labour in a quarry.** Although this photograph was not taken at Auschwitz, it shows exactly the kind of work that Auschwitz prisoners also carried out, breaking huge rocks into gravel and trundling the loaded gravel-wagons to waiting lorries.

Guards and "Trusties"

Hard labour was not the only work done by prisoners. To reduce the number of guards required to control the camp, the SS used prisoners to do some of their work for them. They often appointed criminal prisoners as "Kapos", who made sure they retained their few privileges by savagely applying every order.

Two other special roles gave protection for a short time. One was to work in the "Sonderkommando". Its main job was to collect up and dispose of dead bodies. The Sonderkommando was regularly liquidated and a new group formed. The SS did not want any witnesses to survive.

Some Sonderkommando members managed to thwart the SS and bury evidence of what they had seen. In 1944 they also staged a major sabotage attack that destroyed two of the gas chambers at Auschwitz II.

The other "trusties" role was in "Canada". Canada had a reputation as a land of plenty, so it was the nickname given to the warehouse where the Nazis stored the possessions they had taken from prisoners, on arrival or after they were killed. Those who worked there – the Canadakommando – had to sort all this wealth. Most of them, too, were killed after a time to avoid witnesses.

▼ **Guards on watch.** The camps were run by the SS but many of the guards were locally recruited. Guards like these (this photo was taken at Sachsenhausen concentration camp) manned the watch-towers circling Auschwitz, ready to shoot any prisoner who stepped out of line.

◀ Helping the guards. SS officers in charge of the camp used a number of trusted inmates to help them organise the prisoners arriving at the ramp. The "trusties" can be recognised by their distinctive striped uniform.

▶ "Trusties" among the crowd. Many Auschwitz survivors testify to the fact that "trusties" helping at the selections advised them to claim to be older or say they had a trade. In this tiny piece of resistance, some "trusties" managed to save a few lives.

❝ To work in 'Canada' was the height of prestige because it was the source of all things valuable and useful. Canada was a paradise for 'organising'. Enormous wealth accumulated in these few square miles. When someone knocks on your door and tells you to leave, you take whatever seems most practical: warm clothes, jewellery and the things that are precious to you and might be of some value. So thousands, no, millions of people converged on a relatively small patch of earth carrying their most treasured possessions, and all of these were stolen. ❞
Anita Lasker-Wallfisch

The Doctors at Auschwitz

Auschwitz was also used to conduct medical experiments. In many concentration camps, there were unscrupulous doctors who used prisoners as human guinea pigs. Jews in particular were abused in such experiments – on the grounds that they were "sub-human".

The most infamous SS doctor at Auschwitz was Dr Josef Mengele. Nazis believed in creating a master race; so, like many Nazi scientists, Mengele was fascinated by genetics. He was convinced that conducting experiments on twins would help his research. He and his colleagues also routinely experimented with sterilising women prisoners as part of the Nazis' plans to eradicate entire nations in this way.

If an arriving prisoner was found to be a doctor, he or she was sometimes offered the chance to work on these experiments. It was a particularly cruel choice for a doctor to face. Some agreed in the hope that they could make things better for the victims.

Experiments in Auschwitz were conducted without anaesthetic or concern for the patient's survival. After undergoing such experiments, being selected to "live" must have had a very bitter quality.

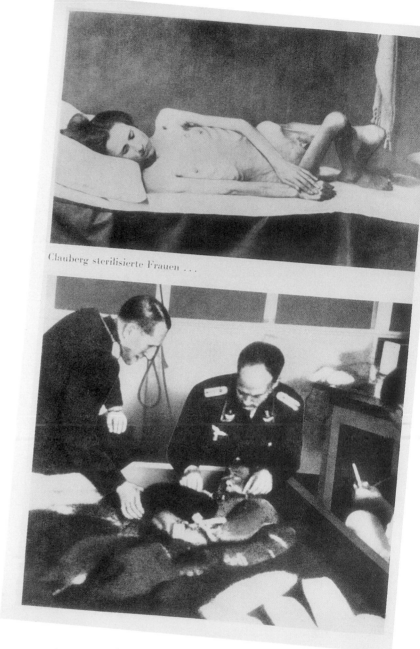

Clauberg sterilisierte Frauen . . .

▲ **Nazi medical experiments.**
A number of doctors worked at Auschwitz, using selected prisoners as guinea pigs for their experiments. Particular attention was paid to genetic experiments on twins, and also the sterilisation of women.

◀ **Entrance to the hospital block.** This is where the medical experiments were carried out. Other prisoners were also treated here if it seemed likely they might survive and provide further useful labour.

HAFTL.-KRANKENBAU
CHIRURGISCHE – ABT.
EINTRITT VERBOTEN

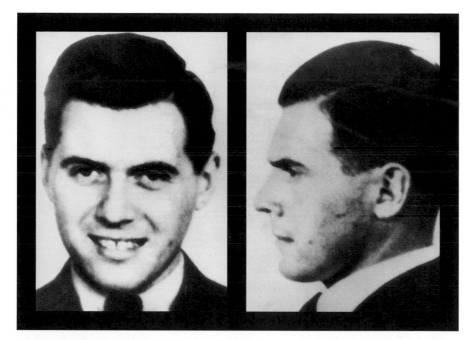

▶ **Dr Josef Mengele.** Mengele presided over medical experiments on women and children. He was also credited with helping to make the gassing system at Auschwitz more scientifically effective.

▼ **Searching for twins.** Mengele was often in attendance when new transports arrived, helping with the selection process. In particular, he was on the lookout for twins on whom he could experiment.

66 I was deported to Auschwitz in January 1943 because, while I was living in France, I insisted on wearing a Yellow Star in sympathy with the Jews. When I arrived at Auschwitz they found I was a psychiatrist and transferred me to the medical block to carry out operations. Dr Wirths, an SS doctor, wanted me to sterilise women but I refused. He was surprised that a psychiatrist would disagree with a method that he was sure would improve the race. 99 Dr Adelaide Hautval

33

▲ **US planes bomb Auschwitz factories, 1944.** As the tide of war turned, the Allies bombed the factories near Auschwitz to stop the production of materials used in the German war effort.

❝ *In January, Auschwitz was liquidated. They marched us out with the children's group in front. After about 10 hours walking, the children began to fall back. But whoever sat down was shot. We three boys developed a system for resting. We ran to the front and then almost stopped, until the back caught up with us. By that time we had rested, and then we ran up again and stayed warm. Suddenly, they stopped the column and told all the children that we were going to a farm. We three didn't go. The children were then taken away, and apparently shot. Only the three of us survived.* ❞

Thomas Burgenthal

The Russians Are Coming!

◀ **The Russian advance.** As the Soviet army pushed the Nazis out of Poland, they were greeted as victorious liberators by the Poles.

In 1944 American warplanes bombed the IG Farben factory. Many wanted the railway lines into Auschwitz to be bombed as well, to stop any more transports, but the Allies argued that this was not the best use of their resources.

Even though they faced certain defeat, the Nazis deliberately chose to speed up the killing at Auschwitz – in a last-ditch attempt to achieve their "Final Solution". Hitler's war against the USSR was going particularly badly. Each side had been totally ruthless, and both Russian and German soldiers knew that they could expect no mercy from the other. By the end of 1944, Soviet troops had entered Poland. As the Russian army advanced, the Nazis made desperate attempts to destroy all evidence of what had been done at Auschwitz. The gas chambers were blown up, thousands of prisoners were killed and most of the remainder were marched west towards Germany.

One of the mysteries of Auschwitz is why its commanders chose to slow their retreat by marching these prisoners across Europe. For the prisoners, already exhausted and malnourished, the forced march was another cruel twist in their ordeal. The challenge of walking hundreds of miles along icy roads, in ill-fitting clogs or without shoes at all, was too much for many of them and they died on the road.

▶ Prisoners await liberation. When the Nazis fled Auschwitz, they left behind some of the slave labourers and a number of children. These were the people the Russian army found when they reached the camp on 27th January 1945.

Liberation

On 27th January 1945, Soviet forces finally reached Auschwitz. They were revolted by what they found. Most people nowadays have seen pictures of the Holocaust, but in 1945 it was a totally new horror. A handful of half-alive prisoners were still there, but otherwise the Russians found a deserted camp with hundreds of empty barrack buildings, half-destroyed crematoria, and piles of bodies which the Nazis had not had time to bury or burn.

Immediately, the Soviet army press-ganged their German prisoners into clearing up the bodies, which had to be done at great speed because of the fear of typhus and other diseases.

Slowly, as more and more camps were liberated at the end of the war, the full scale of the Nazi atrocity became apparent. Even though rumours had circulated as early as 1942 as to what was going on in Auschwitz – and by 1943 actual reports were confirming those rumours – hardly anyone had been able to imagine the reality and scale of this industrial-style murder.

Some continued to try to cover up what had happened. The Kapos were afraid of being accused of collaborating so they were generally not prepared to talk about what had gone on. Many of them changed their names and tried to pretend that they too had been victims.

▶ **Dead bodies frozen in the snow**. Auschwitz was evacuated so quickly that large numbers of bodies were left behind. Many inmates died in the last hours of waiting and were found lying frozen in the snow.

> **❝** *I remember opening the door of a large shed, which they called Canada. It was piled high with suitcases. There was suitcase after suitcase full of children's glasses, and I remember thinking: when the Germans murdered little children, they didn't even throw away their glasses. They kept them to use them again. And the hair: I saw all this hair, women's hair, all colours, and I wondered: how many women do you have to murder to collect that much hair?* **❞** Commander of Russian liberating forces

▼ **Clearing up.** Vast mass funerals were arranged for all the bodies found lying in and around Auschwitz. Local people and German prisoners of war were pressed into service. The locals who were questioned by Soviet officials claimed they had no idea about what had been going on at the camp.

▲ **Walking to freedom.** Many of the liberated prisoners were too weak to stand by themselves, and needed the help of Russian soldiers to be able to walk out of the gates.

What Happened Next?

After the war, many survivors returned home. But most Jewish survivors could not. Their non-Jewish neighbours had frequently stood by or even helped the Nazis capture them. So many Jews were left unwanted, homeless, scattered, ill and poor.

Special "DP" camps were set up for all the "displaced persons" who no longer had a home to go to. The victorious Allies attempted to nurse them back to normality. Generally, the victims wanted to forget what had happened to them and move on. But the experience left deep psychological scars as well as tattooed numbers on their arms.

Meanwhile, many SS officers and camp guards hid or fled abroad. Twenty-one Nazi leaders were tried at Nuremberg in 1945-46 for crimes against humanity. Nearly 3,000 tons of documents, the Nazis' record of what they had done, helped to condemn most of them.

Adolf Eichmann, who masterminded the system for destroying European Jewry, had visited Auschwitz in 1944 to accelerate the killing of Hungarian Jews. He fled to South America, as did Josef Mengele. Mengele died an old man, but Eichmann was kidnapped in 1959, taken to Israel and put on public trial. He claimed he was only following orders and had never personally murdered anybody. This was considered an inadequate defence, and he was found guilty and executed.

▲ **Eichmann on trial, 1961.** Adolf Eichmann, in a bullet-proof box, stands trial in Jerusalem, Israel. His public trial, which started some 15 years after the liberation of Auschwitz, reminded the world of the terrible atrocities that had happened there.

▶ **Children in a DP camp, 1949.**
After the war large numbers of children needed educating in basic behaviour and hygiene. These children had never used soap before.

▶ **A survivors' reunion.**
These four Auschwitz survivors gathered in London in 1964. They have their arms outstretched to show their prisoner numbers tattooed on them.

▶ **The United States' Holocaust Memorial Museum in Washington.** Throughout the 1980s and '90s, considerable efforts were made to record all the facts about the Holocaust before the remaining survivors died. One of the finest and most comprehensive records is to be found in the Holocaust Museum in Washington DC.

39

▼ **International ceremony for Auschwitz survivors.** In 1995 a multinational gathering of survivors marked the 50th anniversary of the liberation of Auschwitz. These people are determined that the world will never forget or misrepresent what happened here.

▼ **Two survivors remember.** These two Polish sisters cry as they remember their own suffering and that of their loved ones at a commemoration of the liberation of the Bergen Belsen camp.

◄ **White Power demonstration in California, USA, 1974.** The White Power movement adopted many Nazi ideas and symbols in its fight against racial integration.

40

Denial

After the war, the appalling evidence found at Auschwitz and other camps forced Nazi sympathisers to keep their opinions to themselves. As time passed, however, the shock began to fade. Old Nazi ideas started to resurface. In many cases the memory of the horror of Auschwitz could still silence them – and the capture and trial of Eichmann in 1959-61 reminded the whole world about the Holocaust.

But, by the mid 1960s, in America, Europe and the Middle East, various groups were ignoring all the evidence and starting to argue that the Jews had invented the story of the Holocaust in order to gain international sympathy.

Modern Nazis knew they had to destroy the memory of Auschwitz in people's minds. They argued that eyewitnesses were now too old to trust; that, without photographs of the gas chambers in action, there was no proof of their existence; that, since no-one could say for sure exactly how many people had died, why believe any figures?

These people need to deny that the Holocaust happened because no decent person who knows the facts can ever again have sympathy with the ideas that the Nazis preached. Again and again, in different court cases around the world, these Holocaust deniers have been proved to be liars and cheats.

▶ **A neo-Nazi demonstration in Germany, 1999.** These protesters are demonstrating against immigrants being given German citizenship. There are still some people who believe that love of their own country means that they should hate all foreigners. Many of them have adopted Nazi ideas. They preach hatred against anybody who is different to them, and continue to see Jews as their fundamental enemy.

Auschwitz Today

While the Communists were in power in Poland (1945-89), they usually presented Auschwitz as a story of particularly Polish suffering. Only recently has it come to represent, more accurately perhaps, the most extreme point of the anti-semitism that raged through Europe in the last century.

Auschwitz itself is now facing many dilemmas.

Those who look after the site want people to visit it so that they can learn about what happened there. At the same time, however, they do not want it to become just another tourist attraction.

▲ **Tourism.** Crowds of tourists wander along one of the ramps on which a million or more prisoners awaited their fate after being unloaded from the cattle trucks.

▶ **Christian claims.** A group of Polish trade unionists erect a 2-metre high cross in front of Auschwitz to stress the scale of Christian suffering that also happened there.

Many Christians died in Auschwitz, including Catholic priests who opposed Nazism in Poland. Although their numbers were small compared to the many Jews killed, some Catholics wish to erect large Christian memorials to them. Jews feel this would misrepresent what Auschwitz was mainly about.

Meanwhile, the people of Oswiecim want to develop their town and look forward. But each time they suggest building a nightclub or a supermarket near the remains of the death camp, the world understandably shudders at the thought of such life-celebrating activities so close to the site of such gigantic murder.

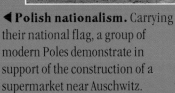

◄ **Polish nationalism.** Carrying their national flag, a group of modern Poles demonstrate in support of the construction of a supermarket near Auschwitz.

▲ **Israeli visitors.** Israelis visit Auschwitz to remember what happened when there was no Jewish state. To them, carrying an Israeli flag there is an act of defiance in the face of history.

How Do We Know?

It is important to remember that Auschwitz was not the only death camp the Nazis built. There were several others, including Belzec, Chelmo, Majdanek, Sobibor and Treblinka, all in Poland. Auschwitz has become a symbol because it was the largest camp where the largest number were killed; also, because of the speed of the Russian advance, the Nazis did not have time to destroy it as they had some of the others.

Auschwitz was a vast complex and, between 1941 and 1945, several million people passed through it. Yet the Nazis did not advertise its existence. Photography was totally banned, and those prisoners who witnessed the worst of what went on were regularly killed.

Before the Nazis fled Auschwitz, they destroyed the gas chambers and most of the documentary records. They knew these were incriminating evidence. However, other sources of information have survived that reveal the extent of the horror.

The buildings

Building plans, aerial photographs and the parts of the camp still standing enable experts to work out its scale and its processes. Although the gas chambers were blown up, they can tell what the buildings were for from the position of their remains. Detailed plans exist showing how they operated. Gas chambers at other camps have survived, showing what is missing at Auschwitz.

Nazi documents and witnesses

The Nazis' ideas and their policy about the Jews are well-documented. For example, full records exist of the 1942 Wannsee conference, at which plans were finalised for exterminating all the Jews of Europe, and which called for a "large killing machine in the East".

The actions of Eichmann and his subsequent testimony also provide evidence. In 1944, his role was crucial in speeding up the deportation of Hungarian Jews, even though Germany was losing the war. Why this eagerness to send them all to Auschwitz, unless it was to kill them? At his trial, Eichmann never attempted to deny that millions had been killed at Auschwitz. He merely denied that he was responsible for it.

The survivors

Some people did survive. These were mainly the prisoners used for slave labour, brought to Auschwitz from all over Europe. Their first-hand testimonies provide some of the most striking evidence, and we have quoted a few in this book.

They all knew that, if they did not keep up with the gruelling demands made on them, they were destined for the gas chambers. Many tell of the continuing stench of burning bodies, non-stop, especially after the arrival of each new transport.

Bodies and "loot"

Although the Nazis burnt a lot before they left, and during the war also sent loads of possessions back to Germany for reuse, there were still huge numbers of bodies and possessions found at Auschwitz when the camp was liberated. The abandoned loot was far in excess of the numbers of prisoners accounted for.

For example, a total of 836,255 women's coats were found. If you assume that each woman coming to Auschwitz brought one coat with her, and that there were at least as many men and probably more children arriving who would not have women's coats, you can count three million people from this discovery alone. Items like teeth were scattered all around the camp and also provide an indication of the scale of the murder.

Surviving photographs

Despite the Nazis' efforts, some photographs did survive. The Sonderkommando managed to smuggle out seven showing prisoners getting ready for the gas chamber and bodies being sorted. (Two of them are reproduced on pages 20 and 25.) In addition an album of some 200 photos taken at Auschwitz was found at the end of the war by a woman called Lili Jacob.

Ankunft eines Transportzuges

The Story of "Lili Jacob's Album"

Other than for identification purposes (for example, the photos across the centre of pages 14-15), photography at Auschwitz was strictly forbidden. However, in May or June 1944, two SS officers – Bernard Walter, Head of the Auschwitz Identification Office, and his assistant Ernst Hoffman – were given special permission to photograph a transport of mainly Hungarian Jews arriving from Carpatho-Ruthenia.

It is not known why Walter and Hoffman were asked to do this, but it may have been for some SS document that never saw the light of day. The result is an album of about 200 photographs, mainly showing the selection process on the ramp at Auschwitz and also something of what happened to these prisoners afterwards.

The story of how the photographs survived is a strange one. They were pasted into an ordinary photo album which was sent to Germany. There, by a twist of fate, it was picked up at the end of the war by a prisoner, Mrs Lili Jacob, who herself came from the region of Carpatho-Ruthenia.

In 1945 Lili Jacob was a prisoner in the Dora Nordhausen concentration camp in Germany. On 2nd May she was in the camp hospital suffering from typhus when American soldiers arrived to liberate the camp. She and some friends were creeping to safety through the German barracks when she spotted the album. Opening it, the first thing she saw was a photo of the rabbi from her own home town. Lili Jacob fainted! Looking through the album in hospital later, she found several photos showing members of her family, all of whom had been sent to Auschwitz and were never seen again.

Lili Jacob emigrated to the USA and took the album with her as a treasured record of her missing family. Only later did she realise its unique historical value. The album is now deposited at Yad Vashem, the Holocaust memorial in Jerusalem, Israel.

Many of the photographs used in this book come from Lili Jacob's album. Their evocative power enables us to imagine what it must have been like for the countless thousands of other prisoners arriving at the Auschwitz ramp.

Who's Who

Adolf Eichmann

Eichmann was the Supervisor of Jewish and Evacuation Affairs in the SS. When people were not being killed quickly enough, he took charge personally. He was captured in South America in 1959, was put on trial in Jerusalem and executed in 1961.

Reinhard Heydrich
Heydrich built up the Nazi Security Service that became known as the Gestapo. His immediate boss was Himmler. It was Heydrich who convened the Wannsee conference and oversaw the beginning of the methodical mass destruction of the Jews. He was assassinated by Czech resistance fighters in 1942.

Heinrich Himmler
Himmler was Hitler's deputy and the head of the Nazi elite force, the SS. He took great interest in the development of Auschwitz and was the immediate boss of both Eichmann and Heydrich. He was captured at the end of the war, and committed suicide before he could be tried.

Rudolf Hoess
Hoess was a major in the SS and the commandant in charge of Auschwitz for most of the war. At the Wannsee conference in 1942, Hoess suggested that his camp (i.e. Auschwitz) would be a suitable place to try out the "Final Solution". He was hanged at Auschwitz in 1947.

Josef Mengele

Mengele was the most famous of the doctors working at Auschwitz. He carried out numerous experiments on twins in particular, as well as advising on how to make the mass-murder process more efficient. He escaped to Brazil and is said to have died there of natural causes in 1979.

Glossary

Anti-semitism
A form of racism based on hatred of Jews.

Block-elder
Someone in charge of a hut or block of prisoners in a concentration camp.

Canadakommando.

Canadakommando
Teams of Auschwitz prisoners employed to sort through the mountains of belongings that arrived with each transport of prisoners and store them in the "Canada" warehouse (so-called because Canada was considered a land of plenty).

Concentration camp
A prison system designed to contain large numbers of prisoners using the minimum number of guards. Most concentration camps had huts for the prisoners, surrounded by electrified fences and barbed wire, with towers for guards to keep watch. There are still concentration camps in some countries.

Crematorium.

Crematorium (plural "crematoria")
A building with large ovens to burn the dead.

"Final Solution"
A term used by Nazis to describe the murder of all Jews: the "final solution" to what they saw as "the Jewish problem".

Gas chamber ruins.

Gas chamber
A Nazi invention to kill large numbers of people by poison-gas. The gas chambers were disguised as showers. Once they were filled with people and the doors sealed, poison-gas instead of water came through holes in the ceiling.

Holocaust
Holocaust means a massive destruction, usually by fire. The Holocaust refers to the mass destruction of Jews by the Nazis in Europe during the Second World War.

Poison-gas canisters.

Kapo

A prisoner who was used to supervise other prisoners on work-duty. Often Kapos were convicts who enjoyed their power. They were notorious for their cruelty.

Nazi

Short form of National Socialist, the name of the political party founded by Hitler. Nazi ideas include the belief that countries are best ruled by a strong, all-powerful leader, and that some groups of people deserve to be treated differently because of their race. Nazis particularly despised the Jews.

Ramp

The concrete platform leading from the station into the camp on which the selection took place.

Sonderkommando

Teams of prisoners who cleared the dead bodies from the gas chambers at Auschwitz, checking them for valuables and loading them into the crematoria. "Sonder" in German means "special".

SS

Elite troops, originally a bodyguard for the Nazi leaders. They were distinguished by their black shirts and their commitment to Nazi teachings.

USSR

Union of Soviet Socialist Republics, a confederation of socialist/communist republics ruled from Moscow. Also known as the "Soviet Union" and popularly as "Russia". The USSR was disbanded in 1991.

Zyklon B

The type of poison-gas used at Auschwitz. It was based on an insecticide and took the form of pellets which released poisonous prussic acid when exposed to air.

▶ From a plaque at Auschwitz.

Timeline

1933	Hitler and the Nazi party come to power in Germany.
1935	Nuremberg Laws are passed, introducing discrimination against Jews.
1938	Hitler invades Austria.
1939	Hitler invades Czechoslovakia. In September he invades Poland and the Allies declare war. Poland is defeated; 3.3 million Polish Jews come under Nazi rule.
1940	Auschwitz I is opened as a concentration camp. Hitler invades Denmark and Norway, then Belgium and Holland, then France. Ghettoes are established in Poland.
1941	Hitler invades the USSR; 5 million Soviet Jews come under Nazi rule. Auschwitz II (Auschwitz-Birkenau) is opened. First attempts at mass killing with gas.
1942	At Wannsee, the Nazis agree plans for a "Final Solution of the Jewish Problem". Jews from Czechoslovakia and France, Holland, Belgium and Luxembourg are sent to Auschwitz. BBC broadcasts news of mass killings; no action is taken.
1943	Gas chambers are opened at Auschwitz II. Jews from Greece, Italy, Latvia and Austria are deported. Warsaw ghetto uprising is put down.
1944	Eichmann is put in charge of liquidating Hungarian Jews. Allied landings in Normandy and Russian advances on Eastern Front put pressure on Germany. Numbers sent to Auschwitz increase.
1945	Auschwitz is liberated by the Russian army in January. In May the Germans surrender. Hitler commits suicide.
1946	19 Nazis are found guilty of war crimes at the Nuremberg trials.

FOR EVER LET THIS PLACE
BE A CRY OF DESPAIR AND A WARNING TO
HUMANITY, WHERE THE NAZIS MURDERED
ABOUT ONE-AND-A-HALF MILLION MEN,
WOMEN AND CHILDREN, MAINLY JEWS,
FROM VARIOUS COUNTRIES OF EUROPE.

Index

Acknowledgments

Design
M&M Design Partnership

Picture research
Sue Mennell

Photographs
AKG London pp. 6t & b, 7b, 8b, 9t,
10, 11, 12, 13, 14, 14-15 (strip), 15tr-
br (Michael Teller), 16-17b, 17br, 18
(inset), 20, 21t, 23t (Michael Teller),
23b, 25r, 25 (background), 26t, 31t,
34l, 36, 39b (Keith Collie), 45t, 46brb
Axiom pp. 27l (Jiri Rezac), 32b (Jiri
Rezac), 43r (E. Simanor)
Franklin Watts p. 9c (courtesy of the
Imperial War Museum)
Novosti, London pp. 12-13, 24, 25l,
26-27 (background), 34r, 34-35,
36-37, 37, 46trb,
©Panstwowe Muzeum
Auschwitz-Birkenau
pp. 3 (ref. 716/1), 5 (ref. 20 998/21)
Popperfoto pp. 2, 7t, 15t, 16-17t, 29,
30, 39t (Reuters/Reinhard
Krause), 40-41 (Reuters/Peter
Mueller), 41 (Reuters/Jochen Eckel),
42r (Reuters/Pawel Kopczynski),
42-43 (Reuters/Reinhard Krause),
43l (Reuters/Pawel Kopczynski), 46tl
©Rod Shone Cover (t) and pp. 1,
2-3, 4, 4-5
Topham Picturepoint
pp. 8t, 26b, 31b, 32t, 33t, 38, 39c,
42l (J. Finck), 44, 46bl
©Yad Vashem Photo Archive,
Jerusalem
Cover (b), endpapers and pp. 9b, 17t,
18-19, 19 (inset), 21b, 22-23, 27r,
28-29, 33b, 46tra, 46 bra

Quotations and testimonies
The Author and Publishers would
like to thank Andrea Sonkin for her
help in researching the quotations.
Sources include *The Boys* by Martin
Gilbert, published by Weidenfeld &
Nicolson; *The World Must Know* by
Michael Berenbaum, published by
Little, Brown and Company;
Holocaust Journey by Martin
Gilbert, published by Phoenix; and
Inherit the Truth by Anita Lasker-
Wallfisch, published by Giles de la
Mare Publishers.
Other quotations are as told to
the Author.